First World War
and Army of Occupation
War Diary
France, Belgium and Germany

I0270600

60 DIVISION
179 Infantry Brigade
Headquarters
6 September 1915 - 30 November 1916

WO95/3030/2

The Naval & Military Press Ltd
www.nmarchive.com
Published in association with The National Archives

Published by

The Naval & Military Press Ltd

Unit 10 Ridgewood Industrial Park,

Uckfield, East Sussex,

TN22 5QE England

Tel: +44 (0) 1825 749494

www.naval-military-press.com

www.nmarchive.com

This diary has been reprinted in facsimile from the original. Any imperfections are inevitably reproduced and the quality may fall short of modern type and cartographic standards.

Contents

Document type	Place/Title	Date From	Date To
Heading	WO95/3030/2		
Heading	60 Division HQ. 179 Brigade 1915 Sep-1916 May		
War Diary		06/09/1915	03/12/1915
Heading	War Diary Of 179th Infantry Brigade From December 1st 1915 To December 31st 1915 Volume 1.		
War Diary	Bishops Stortford	03/12/1915	20/12/1915
War Diary	Sawbridgeworth	20/12/1915	20/12/1915
War Diary	Ware	21/12/1915	21/12/1915
War Diary	Bishops Stortford	23/12/1915	28/12/1915
Miscellaneous	Appendix A 179th Infantry Brigade.	01/12/1915	01/12/1915
Miscellaneous	179th Infantry Brigade. Concentration March.	07/12/1915	07/12/1915
War Diary	Longbridge Deverill	28/04/1916	29/04/1916
War Diary	Neyland	30/04/1916	01/05/1916
War Diary	Queenstown	02/05/1916	06/05/1916
War Diary	Ballincollig	07/05/1916	07/05/1916
War Diary	Coachford	08/05/1916	08/05/1916
War Diary	Macroom	09/05/1916	12/05/1916
War Diary	Said Hill Camp Longbridge Diverill Wilts	14/06/1916	29/06/1916
War Diary	Ecoivres	30/06/1916	30/06/1916
Miscellaneous	179th Infantry Brigade		
Operation(al) Order(s)	Operation Order No. 110 by Brig General D. Campbell Commanding 153rd Infantry Brigade	28/06/1916	28/06/1916
Miscellaneous	Movement Table		
Heading	War Diary 179th Infantry Brigade Headquarters July 1st 1916-July 31st 1916		
Miscellaneous	3rd Echelon Base	01/07/1916	01/07/1916
War Diary	Ecoivres	01/07/1916	13/07/1916
War Diary	Trenches	13/07/1916	15/07/1916
War Diary	Neuville St Vaast	13/07/1916	15/07/1916
War Diary	Trenches	20/07/1916	31/07/1916
Miscellaneous	Appendix III 179th Infantry Brigade.		
Miscellaneous	Appendix IV Strength Return.	01/07/1916	01/07/1916
Miscellaneous	Strength Return	31/07/1916	31/07/1916
Miscellaneous	179th Infantry Brigade	14/07/1916	14/07/1916
Miscellaneous	179th Infantry Brigade.	15/07/1916	15/07/1916
Miscellaneous	179th Infantry Brigade. Daily Intelligence Summary 10 a.m. 15/7/16 to 10 a.m. 16/7/16	16/07/1916	16/07/1916
Miscellaneous	Daily Intelligence Report.	17/07/1916	17/07/1916
Miscellaneous	179th Infantry Brigade. Daily Intelligence Report 10 a.m. 17/7/16 to 10 a.m. 18/7/16.	18/07/1916	18/07/1916
Miscellaneous	179th Infantry Brigade. Weekly Intelligence Summary.	18/07/1916	18/07/1916
Miscellaneous	179th Infantry Brigade. Daily Intelligence Summary 10 a.m. 18/7/16 to 10 a.m. 19/7/16	19/07/1916	19/07/1916
Miscellaneous	179th Infantry Brigade. Daily Intelligence Summary 10 a.m. 19/7/16 to 10 a.m. 20/7/16	20/07/1916	20/07/1916
Miscellaneous	179th Infantry Brigade. Daily Intelligence Summary 10 a.m. 20/7/16 to 10 a.m. 21/7/16	21/07/1916	21/07/1916
Miscellaneous	179th Infantry Brigade. Daily Intelligence Summary 10 a.m. 21/7/16 to 10 a.m. 22/7/16	22/07/1916	22/07/1916

Miscellaneous	179th Infantry Brigade. Daily Intelligence Summary 10 a.m. 22/7/16 to 10 a.m. 23/7/16	23/07/1916	23/07/1916
Miscellaneous	179th Infantry Brigade. Daily Intelligence Summary 10 a.m. 23/7/16 to 10 a.m. 24/7/16	24/07/1916	24/07/1916
Miscellaneous	179th Infantry Brigade. Daily Intelligence Summary 10 a.m. 24/7/16 to 10 a.m. 25/7/16	25/07/1916	25/07/1916
Miscellaneous	179th Infantry Brigade Weekly Intelligence Summary.	25/07/1916	25/07/1916
Miscellaneous	179th Infantry Brigade. Daily Intelligence Summary 10 a.m. 25/7/16 to 10 a.m. 26/7/16	26/07/1916	26/07/1916
Miscellaneous	179th Infantry Brigade. Daily Intelligence Summary 10 a.m. 26/7/16 to 10 a.m. 27/7/16	27/07/1916	27/07/1916
Miscellaneous	179th Infantry Brigade. Daily Intelligence Summary 10 a.m. 27/7/16 to 10 a.m. 28/7/16	28/07/1916	28/07/1916
Miscellaneous	179th Infantry Brigade. Daily Intelligence Summary 10 a.m. 28/7/16 to 10 a.m. 29/7/16	29/07/1916	29/07/1916
Miscellaneous	179th Infantry Brigade. Daily Intelligence Summary 10 a.m. 29/7/16 to 10 a.m. 30/7/16	30/07/1916	30/07/1916
Miscellaneous	179th Infantry Brigade	31/07/1916	31/07/1916
Map	Map		
Miscellaneous	179th Bde July 1916		
Heading	War Diary Of 179th Infantry Brigade From 1st August 1916 Vol 3		
War Diary	Trenches Near Neuville St Vaast	01/08/1916	31/08/1916
Miscellaneous	179th Infantry Brigade. Weekly Intelligence Summary.	09/08/1916	09/08/1916
Miscellaneous	179th Infantry Brigade. Weekly Intelligence Summary.	16/08/1916	16/08/1916
Miscellaneous	179th Infantry Brigade Weekly Intelligence Summary.	23/08/1916	23/08/1916
Miscellaneous	179th Infantry Brigade. Weekly Intelligence Summary.	30/08/1916	30/08/1916
Miscellaneous	Headquarters, 60th (London) Division	07/08/1916	07/08/1916
Miscellaneous	Report By Lieut W. Read 2/13th London Regiment 8/8/16	08/08/1916	08/08/1916
Operation(al) Order(s)	179th Infantry Brigade Operation Order No. 6		
Diagram etc	Diagram		
Miscellaneous	Trench Mortar Programme		
Miscellaneous	179th Infantry Brigade	11/08/1916	11/08/1916
Miscellaneous	Copy	23/08/1916	23/08/1916
Map	Map		
Miscellaneous	Appendix VII Raid by 2/4th Battalion London Regiment.	26/08/1916	26/08/1916
Miscellaneous	Appendix IX 179th Infantry Brigade.		
Miscellaneous	Appendix X 179th Infantry Brigade.	01/08/1916	01/08/1916
Miscellaneous	179th Infantry Brigade Appendix X	31/08/1916	31/08/1916
Heading	War Diary 179th Inf. Bde. From 1st Sept 1916 To 30th Sept 1918		
War Diary	Neuville St Vaast Trenches	01/09/1916	30/09/1916
Miscellaneous	Appendix XII C.O.C. 179th Infantry Brigade.	11/09/1916	11/09/1916
Miscellaneous	Statement By Lieut B. Peatfield	11/09/1916	11/09/1916
Miscellaneous	Statement By 2/Lieut Thompson	11/09/1916	11/09/1916
Map	Map		
Miscellaneous	Appendix XIII Report on Raid Carried out in Accordance With My Operation Order No.20 dated 21st September 1916	24/09/1916	24/09/1916
Miscellaneous	Appendix XIV Report on Raid Carried out by the 2nd Bn. London Scottish on the German front Line in Accordance With My Operation Orders No.1		
Map	Map		
Miscellaneous	Report Of Support Party	30/09/1916	30/09/1916

Miscellaneous	Report On Raid Carried Out By 2/14th Bn London Regt (London Scottish) On The night 29th/30th September 1916	30/09/1918	30/09/1918
Miscellaneous	Appendix		
Miscellaneous	Appendix XV 179th Infantry Brigade.		
Miscellaneous	Appendix XVI 179th Infantry Brigade.	01/09/1916	01/09/1916
Miscellaneous	179th Infantry Brigade Strength Return	30/09/1916	30/09/1916
Miscellaneous	Appendix XVII 179th Infantry Brigade.	05/09/1916	05/09/1916
Miscellaneous	179th Infantry Brigade Weekly Intelligence Summary For Week ending September 12th 1916	12/09/1916	12/09/1916
Miscellaneous	179th Infantry Brigade Weekly Intelligence Summary For Week Ending September 19th 1916	19/06/1916	19/06/1916
Miscellaneous	179th Infantry Brigade Weekly Intelligence Summary For Week Ending September 26th 1916	27/09/1916	27/09/1916
Heading	179th Infantry Brigade Headquarters War Diary Volume 5 October 1916		
War Diary	Trenches Neuville St Vaast	01/10/1916	25/10/1916
War Diary	Ecoivres	26/10/1916	26/10/1916
War Diary	Buneville	27/10/1916	29/10/1916
War Diary	Ribeaucourt	30/10/1916	31/10/1916
Miscellaneous	Appendix XXII 179th Infantry Brigade.	03/10/1916	03/10/1916
Miscellaneous	179th Infantry Brigade Weekly Intelligence Summary For week ending October 10th 1916	10/10/1916	10/10/1916
Miscellaneous	179th Infantry Brigade Weekly Intelligence Summary For week ending October 17th 1916	17/10/1916	17/10/1916
Miscellaneous	179th Infantry Brigade Weekly Intelligence Summary For Week Ending October 24th 1916	24/10/1916	24/10/1916
Operation(al) Order(s)	179th Infantry Brigade Operation Order No. 19	20/10/1916	20/10/1916
Miscellaneous	Table		
Miscellaneous	Appendix "A"		
Miscellaneous	Appendix "B" Advanced Parties.		
Miscellaneous	Appendix "C" Billeting Parties		
Miscellaneous	179th Infantry Brigade	22/10/1916	22/10/1916
Miscellaneous	March Table		
Miscellaneous	Amendment To 179th Brigade T.123/20	22/10/1916	22/10/1916
Operation(al) Order(s)	179th Infantry Brigade Operation Orders No.20	25/10/1916	25/10/1916
Miscellaneous	Route Frevent Vacquerie Le Boucq		
Operation(al) Order(s)	179th Infantry Brigade Operation Orders No.21	27/10/1916	27/10/1916
Operation(al) Order(s)	179th Infantry Brigade Operation Orders No.22	28/10/1916	28/10/1916
Miscellaneous	Appendix XXIV 179th Infantry Brigade.	30/09/1916	30/09/1916
Heading	War Diary Of 179th Inf Bde Hdqrs For November 1st-30th 1916		
War Diary	Ribeaucourt	01/11/1916	03/11/1916
War Diary	Bellancourt	04/11/1916	17/11/1916
War Diary	Marseilles	18/11/1916	19/11/1916
War Diary	At Sea	20/11/1916	30/11/1916
War Diary	Salonica	30/11/1916	30/11/1916
Miscellaneous	Appendix XXIII 179th Infantry Brigade.	01/10/1916	01/10/1916
Operation(al) Order(s)	179th Infantry Brigade Operation Orders No.23	02/11/1916	02/11/1916
Miscellaneous	March Table		
Operation(al) Order(s)	179th Infantry Brigade Operation Orders No.24	13/11/1916	13/11/1916
Miscellaneous	179th Infantry Brigade Longpre To Marseilles		
Miscellaneous	179th Infantry Brigade Transport To Be Return		
Miscellaneous	179th Infantry Brigade Strength Return	01/11/1916	01/11/1916
Miscellaneous	179th Infantry Brigade	30/11/1916	30/11/1916

60 DIVISION

HQ 179 BRIGADE

1915 SEP – 1916 MAY

60 DIV

Instructions regarding War Diaries and Intelligence Summaries are contained in F. S. Regs., Part II. and the Staff Manual respectively. Title pages will be prepared in manuscript.

WAR DIARY

or

~~INTELLIGENCE SUMMARY~~.

(Erase heading not required.)

179th INFANTRY BRIGADE. No. .... Date 4 Octo 1915

Army Form C. 2118.

Period 5th September to 4th October inclusive.

Place	Date	Hour	Summary of Events and Information	Remarks and references to Appendices
	6/9/15.		Brigade Convoy Attack.	
	9/9/15.		Lt.General Cmdg. Third Army inspected Bombing School.	
			Inspected Composite Battalions, A.S.C.Co. & Field Ambulance.	
	13/9/15.		Brigade Tactical Scheme - Outpost Lines.	
	15/9/15.		Units practice Entraining and Detraining, at Saffron Walden Station. This practice continued until the 18th instant.	
	16/9/15.		O.C., A.S.C. inspects Transport.	
	17/9/15.		Night Operations - Attackb at Dawn by 2/14th Battalion.	
	18/9/15.		2/13th & 2/14th Battalions ordered to send three Officers Overseas, for reinforcements.	
	23/9/15.		Inspection of Mobile Column by G.O.C., 60th (London) Division.	
	27-28/9/15.		Brigade Tactical Training - Night Bivouac.	
	29/9/15.		Representative of Ministry of Munitions addressed the Brigade with a view to obtaining Recruits for Munition Work.	
	30/9/15.		Saw two Battalions Assaulting out of Trenches, taking first and second Line.	
	1/10/15.		Saw other two Battalions Assaulting out of Trenches, taking first and second Line.	

E W Baird

COLONEL, Cmdg.179th Infantry Brigade.

1577 Wt. W10791/1773 500,000 1/15 D. D. & L. A.D.S.S./Forms/C. 2118.

Instructions regarding War Diaries and Intelligence Summaries are contained in F. S. Regs., Part II. and the Staff Manual respectively. Title pages will be prepared in manuscript.

WAR DIARY
or
INTELLIGENCE SUMMARY.

(*Erase heading not required.*)

Army Form C. 2118.

Period 5th September to 4th October inclusive.

Place	Date	Hour	Summary of Events and Information	Remarks and references to Appendices
	6/9/15.		Brigade Convoy Attack.	
	9/9/15.		Lt.General Cmdg. Third Army inspected Bombing School.	
			Inspected Composite Battalions, A.S.C.Co. & Field Ambulance.	
	13/9/15.		Brigade Tactical Scheme - Outpost Lines.	
	15/9/15.		Units practice Entraining and Detraining, at Saffron Walden Station. This practice continued until the 18th instant.	
	16/9/15.		O.C., A.S.C. inspects Transport.	
	17/9/15.		Night Operations - Attackb at Dawn by 2/14th Battalion.	
	18/9/15.		2/13th & 2/14th Battalions ordered to send three Officers Overseas, for reinforcements.	
	23/9/15.		Inspection of Mobile Column by G.O.C., 60th (London) Division.	
	27-28/9/15.		Brigade Tactical Training - Night Bivouac.	
	29/9/15.		Representative of Ministry of Munitions addressed the Brigade with a view to obtaining Recruits for Munition Work.	
	30/9/15.		Saw two Battalions Assaulting out of Trenches, taking first and second Line.	
	1/10/15.		Saw other two Battalions Assaulting out of Trenches, taking first and second Line.	

(sd) E. W. BAIRD.

COLONEL, Cmdg.179th Infantry Brigade.

1577 Wt. W10791/1773 500,000 1/15 D. D. & L. A.D.S.S./Forms/C. 2118.

Instructions regarding War Diaries and Intelligence Summaries are contained in F. S. Regs., Part II. and the Staff Manual respectively. Title pages will be prepared in manuscript.

WAR DIARY
or
INTELLIGENCE SUMMARY.

Army Form C. 2118.

(*Erase heading not required.*) Period 5th October to 4th November 1915 inclusive.

Hour, Date, Place	Summary of Events and Information	Remarks and references to Appendices
5/10/15.	The Brigade marched out of Saffron Walden at 6.30 a.m. At 10.50 a.m. 1 hour's halt, for watering horses. Arrived at the Bivouac area at 12.35 p.m. As the Brigade was marching in, it was met by the General Officer Commanding Third Army. The attached Troops 2/5th London Bde. R.F.A. and 3/3rd Field Co. R.E., joined the Brigade at the Bivouac area. The marching of the Brigade this day was good. The Marching out strength of the Brigade was 102 Officers and 1902 men.	
6/10/15.	The Brigade marched out of its Bivouac Area on the 6th. at 8 a.m. At 12 noon the Brigade received orders to take up a defensive position. Operations were suspended at 6 p.m. The Brigade Headquarters moved to Bocking Place for the night.	
7/10/15.	The Brigade left the Billeting Area at 7.30 a.m. and proceeded to Stebbing. All operations ceased on the arrival of the Brigade at Stebbing where they bivouaced for the Night.	
8/10/15.	The Brigade marched to Saffron Walden arriving at 1.40 p.m., the attached Troops having left the bivouac area at 6 a.m.	
12/10/15.	Staff Ride over ground for Divisional Tactical Day on the 14th.	
13/10/15.	Attended conference of G.O.C. Division at Stortford at 2.30 p.m. on the recent manoeuvres.	
14/10/15.	Divisional Tactical Day. Brigade marched out of Saffron Walden at 7.30 a.m. At 10.40 a.m. Rendezvous was arrived at where the Columns were met by Officer s and two men R.E. Guides to convey Battalions to their position in the Trenches. At 1.45 p.m. orders were received from Division that Battalions should advance	

(9 29 6) W 2794 100,000 8/14 H W V Forms/C. 2118/11

Instructions regarding War Diaries and Intelligence Summaries are contained in F. S. Regs., Part II. and the Staff Manual respectively. Title pages will be prepared in manuscript.

WAR DIARY
or
INTELLIGENCE SUMMARY.
(Erase heading not required.)

Army Form C. 2118.

Hour, Date, Place	Summary of Events and Information - 2 -	Remarks and references to Appendices
14/10/15 (contd.)	to the Assault of the Enemy's Trenches. The message was received very late from Division and it was found impossible to notify Battalions from the time the Advance should start so the Advance was not simultaneous. At 2.20 p.m. the G.O.C., 60th (London) Division, started visiting Brigade Headquarters. Operations ceased at this time and Battalions moved to their Bivouac Areas.	
15/10/15.	Brigade returned to Saffron Walden on the morning of the 15th. arriving at 12.30 p.m.	
16/10/15.	O.C., No. 2 Co., A.S.C. Supply Officer left for Southampton for Overseas.	
19/10/15.	Brigade marched out of Saffron Walden for four days Operations. Head of Column passed Starting Point at 10.30 a.m. At 2 p.m. 1 hour's halt for watering horses. At 2.45 p.m. Orders for Night position of Advanced Guard. Outpost to be in position by 5.30 p.m. At 4.30 p.m. Brigade arrived at Stebbing to bivouac for the Night.	
20/10/15.	Head of main body passed starting point at 9.45 a.m. At 9.58 a.m. orders were received from Division to occupy a line of Trenches. At 4.55 p.m. orders received for Units to return to Billets in Braintree.	
21/10/15.	Received orders from G.O.C. Division for Brigade to retire and take up three separate positions. At 2.40 p.m. orders received for Brigade to retire to billeting areas.	
22/10/15.	Brigade marched back to Saffron Walden. At 2.30 p.m. the G.O.C. Division and Staff came over to Walden.	

(9 29 6) W 2794 100,000 8/14 H W V Forms/C. 2118/11

Instructions regarding War Diaries and Intelligence Summaries are contained in F. S. Regs., Part II. and the Staff Manual respectively. Title pages will be prepared in manuscript.

WAR DIARY
or
INTELLIGENCE SUMMARY.
(Erase heading not required.)

Army Form C. 2118.

Hour, Date, Place	Summary of Events and Information	Remarks and references to Appendices
25/10/15.	180th. Brigade marched into Saffron Walden.	
26/10/15.	179th Brigade proceeded to Bishop's Stortford, marching in at 2 p.m. 2/13th. Battalion proceeded to Sawbridgeworth where they will be billeted. The remainder of the Brigade billeted at Bishop's Stortford. The G.O.C. Division came out to Stansted to see the Brigade pass.	
28/10/15.	Colonel Long inspected all Horses of the Brigade at 3 p.m. with a view to casting.	
30/10/15.	2nd/Lieut. T.C.Foster, 2/13th. Battalion, with Detachment proceeded to Hertford for Detached Duty under C.F. They took over their duties on the 31st.	
3/11/15.	One Company 2/14th Battalion proceeded to Hertford on special duty.	
4/11/15.	Divisional Tactical Scheme.	
	E W Baird. COLONEL, Comdg. 179th. Infantry Brigade. 4th. November 1915.	

Instructions regarding War Diaries and Intelligence Summaries are contained in F. S. Regs., Part II. and the Staff Manual respectively. Title pages will be prepared in manuscript.

WAR DIARY
or
INTELLIGENCE SUMMARY.

179th INFANTRY BRIGADE. No. .... Date. ....

Army Form C. 2118.

(Erase heading not required.) Period 5th November to 4th December 1915 inclusive.

Hour, Date, Place	Summary of Events and Information	Remarks and references to Appendices
11/11/15.	Received orders that all Japanese Rifles and Ammunition to be handed in to D.A.D.O.S. .303 Long Rifles were issued to 4 Units under my command.	BL
15/11/15.	Started Brigade Riding School for all Officers and Transport Drivers.	BL
16/11/15.	G.O.C., Division, inspected billets, central feeding & Transport Stables of 2/14th, 2/15th & 2/16th Battalions.	BL
19/11/15.	Inspected 2/13th Battalion on parade. Inspected Adjutant's, Q.M's and Company Officer's books. Also Central Feeding.	BL
22/11/15.	2/14th Battalion practised Entraining and Detraining.	BL
23/11/15.	2/16th Battalion practised Entraining and Detraining.	BL
25/11/15.	Inspected 2/14th Battalion on parade. Inspected Adjutant's, Q.M's and Company Officer's books. Also Central Feeding.	BL
26/11/15.	2/15th Battalion practised Entraining and Detraining. Attended final day of Bombing School Classes. Much pleased with the work and keenness shown by the men.	BL
29/11/15.	2/15th Battalion proceeded to Ware. BL	
30/11/15.	Detachments of 2/14th Battalion at Hertford and 2/13th Battalion at Hertford Heath were relieved by the 2/15th Battalion.	BL
2/12/15.	2/13th Battalion practised Entraining and Detraining. BL.	
3/12/15.	Inspected 2/16th Battalion on parade. Inspected Adjutant's, Q.M's and Company Officer's books. Also Central Feeding.	BL.

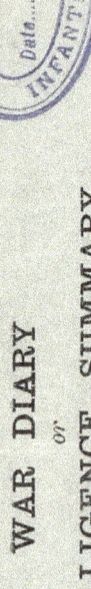

E W Baird
COLONEL.
COMDG 179th INF. BDE.

(9 29 6) W2794 100,000 8/14 H W V Forms/C. 2118/11

C O N F I D E N T I A L

War Diary of

179th Infantry Brigade

from December 1st 1915 to December 31st 1915.

Volume 1.

Instructions regarding War Diaries and Intelligence Summaries are contained in F. S. Regs., Part II. and the Staff Manual respectively. Title pages will be prepared in manuscript.

WAR DIARY
or
INTELLIGENCE SUMMARY.
(Erase heading not required.)

Army Form C. 2118.

Hour, Date, Place		Summary of Events and Information	Remarks and references to Appendices
3.12.15	BISHOPS. STORTFORD	Inspected 2/16th Battn 1st line transport and all stables. also Battn & Coy books: visited Battn at Central feeding	excellent. BL
4.12.15	"	Issued orders to 2/13. 2/14, 2/15th Battns Lon. Regt for a Bde concentration march	BL. Appendix A
6.12.15	"	Received orders from 60th Lon Divn for all officers retained with 2nd line units to be medically examined for service overseas.	authority 60th Lon Divn No 1517/16 A BL
7.12.15	"	Bde concentration march: The Lt Genl Comg 3rd Army met the Bde at pt of concentration: inspected the three battns and drew attention to the weakness of battns on parade: strength 880.	BL
9.12.15	"	Inspected 2/15th Battn on parade strength offrs 20. OR. 429	turn out & marching of battn good
		Inspected Battn and Coy books. Visited battn at Central feeding	books v. good: feeding excellent BL
14.12.15	"	Inspected 1st line transport 2/14th Battn	BL
17.12.15	"	Inspected 2/16th Battn on parade strength 20 offrs 447 OR.	v. good
		Inspected 1st line transport strength offrs 2. horses 45	v. good. BL
18.12.15	"	Inspected Stables No 2 Coy. Signal Section	clean. horses in good condition BL
19.12.15.	"	Maj Genl E. S. Bulfin C.V.O. C.B. assumed command 60th Lon Divn vice Brig. Genl. J. C. P. Colley C.B. MVO.	authority W.O. telegram 6061 (AG 4) dated 16-12-15 BL

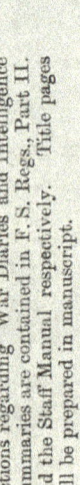

(9 29 6) W2794 100,000 8/14 H W V Forms/C. 2118/11

Instructions regarding War Diaries and Intelligence Summaries are contained in F. S. Regs., Part II. and the Staff Manual respectively. Title pages will be prepared in manuscript.

WAR DIARY
or
INTELLIGENCE SUMMARY.
(Erase heading not required.)

179th INFANTRY BRIGADE. No. .... Date ....

Army Form C. 2118.

Hour, Date, Place	Summary of Events and Information	Remarks and references to Appendices
20. 12. 15. BISHOPS. STORTFORD 9.30. a. m	G.O.C. 60th Lon Div inspected 2/14th Batt Lon. Regt and 1st line transport. Strength officers 24. O.R. 534.	BL
" " " 10.15 a m "	G.O.C. 60th Lon. Div inspected 2/16th Batt Lon. Regt and 1st line transport. Strength officers 20. O.R. 494.	BL
" " " 11.15 a m SAWBRIDGEWORTH.	G.O.C 60th Lon Div inspected 2/13th Battn Lon Regt and 1st line transport	BL
21-12-15. 11. a. m WARE	G.O.C. 60th Lon. Div inspected 2/15th Batt Lon. Regt and 1st line transport	BL
23. 12. 15. BISHOPS STORTFORD.	Inspected Central feeding and Kitchens 2/14th Battn	BL
24. 12 15. "	Captain R.P. Gladstone 2/13th Batt detailed as officer Comg Div Supply Col.	authority 60th L. Div no 140/C BL
25. 12 15 "	Xmas Day. Parade Service.	BL
28. 12. 15. "	Col. E.W. Baird Comg 179th Inf. Bde. Lt Col. C.A. Gordon-Clark Comg 2/16th Battn proceed to France to spend three days at Hd Qrs BEF.	BL.
	Lt Col. W.R.J. Maclean Comg 2/13th Battn assumes Command of 179th Inf Bde in addition to his other duties during the absence on duty of Col. E.W. Baird	BL

W R J McLean Lt Col
for Colonel Comdt 179th Infy Bde.

(9 29 6) W2794 100,000 8/14 H W V Forms/C. 2118/11

Appendix "A"

Concentration March, 7th December 1915

179th Infantry Brigade.

ORDERS

by

COLONEL E. W. BAIRD, COMMANDING.

....

179th Infantry Brigade.

CONCENTRATION MARCH.

Tuesday, 7th December, 1915.

Reference:- Ord. Survey Training Sheet No. 29 1 inch - 2 miles.

BISHOP'S STORTFORD.
4th December 1915.

The 179th Infantry Brigade will concentrate on LITTLE HADHAM - WIDFORD Road facing SOUTH - head of column at Road Junction WEST of C in HADHAM CROSS. at 12 o'clock noon on Tuesday, 7th December 1915, in the following order:-

2/15th Battalion.
2/13th Battalion.
2/14th Battalion.

Companies will concentrate to Battalions at the following points:-

2/13th Battalion concentration point - Road bend WEST of first T in THORLEY STREET.
2/14th Battalion concentration point - Cross Roads SOUTH of O in STANDON.
2/15th Battalion concentration point - Road junction EAST of Point 182 on BARWICK - HADHAM CROSS Road.

Transport fully loaded will accompany Battalions, sufficient being left behind to deal with supplies.

A haversack ration will be carried.

BY ORDER.

B. LEVETT.

Captain & Brigade Major,
179th Infantry Brigade.

Appendix "B".

Instructions regarding War Diaries and Intelligence Summaries are contained in F. S. Regs., Part II. and the Staff Manual respectively. Title pages will be prepared in manuscript.

WAR DIARY

or

~~INTELLIGENCE SUMMARY~~.

(*Erase heading not required.*)

Army Form C. 2118.

Place	Date	Hour	Summary of Events and Information	Remarks and references to Appendices
			April 1916	
Longbridge Deverill.	28.4.16.	2.30 p.m.	Received Orders for 2/16th Battalion to proceed to Ireland fully armed and equipped, 300 rounds S.A.A. per men to be taken. All transport, 3 days supplies and 1 blanket per man. The Battalion marched out 22 Officers and 702 Other Ranks under Lieut.Col.Gordon Clark, and entrained at Warminster in 3 trains scheduled to leave at 6, 6.30 and 7.30 p.m. Each train was somewhat late in starting owing to supply Wagons being late in arriving at Battalion Headquarters.	
		7.30 p.m	Orders received for remainder of Brigade to entrain for Ireland.	
Longbridge Deverill.	29.4.16.		These Battalions left Warminster Station in 5 trained and detrained at NEYLAND. First train arrived NEYLAND 11.15 a.m. Second train " " 12.15 p.m. Third " " " 1.30 p.m. Fourth " " " 2.45 p.m. Brigade accommodated under canvas. The 2/16th Battalion who arrived at 3.0 a.m. embarked 2 Companies on S.S.ARCHANGEL which sailed at 4.15 p.m. Remainder of 2/16th Battalion on S.S.INNESFALLEN.	Marchin Out State, Appendix I
Neyland.	30.4.16.		S.S.ARCHANGEL sailed at 11.15 a.m. with troop as in Appendix II. S.S.SNOWDEN was loaded with part of 2/13th with complete transport. Difficulty was experienced in loading G.S.Wagons as drivers seats with brake handles had to be removed before they could be placed between decks. The ship left the quay side at 5.15 and anchored off Pembroke Dock.	
	1.5.16.		Troops as in Appendix II embarked on S.S.RATHMORE and S.S.ARCHANGEL which had returned from Cork and at 7.0 p.m. under escort of a destroyer left the Haven in company with S.S.SNOWDEN.	
Queenstown	2.5.16.		Convoy arrived at Queenstown at 4.0 a.m. Troops disembarked at 7.0 a.m. and marched to Fota Park, a distance of 5 miles where the 2/16th Battalion were already encamped. Tents and Camp Equipment were drawn for 13th, 14th and 15th Battalions, but at 12 noon orders were received for 2/16th to proceed to LIMERICK so the 2/15th occupied their camp. The 2/16th left for Limerick at 8.0 p.m.	

1577 Wt. W10791/1773 500,000 1/15 D. D. & L. A.D.S.S./Forms/C. 2118.

Army Form C. 2118.

Instructions regarding War Diaries and Intelligence Summaries are contained in F. S. Regs., Part II. and the Staff Manual respectively. Title pages will be prepared in manuscript.

WAR DIARY
or
INTELLIGENCE SUMMARY.
(Erase heading not required.)

Place	Date	Hour	Summary of Events and Information	Remarks and references to Appendices
Queenstown	3.5.16		Morning spent improving conveniences of the camp and Physical Training. In the afternoon at 3.30 H.T. Innesfallen was reported to have arrived at Queenstown with the remainder of the Brigade which had been left at NEYLAND.	Appendix II.
	4.5.16.		Remained in Camp at FOTA.	
	5.5.16.		Remained in Camp at FOTA. Handed in all surplus ordnance stores only keeping suffcient tents for use on mobile column i.e. 1 to 3 Officers and 1 for 12 men.	
	6.5.16		Marched at 8.30 a.m. (Marching Out State - Appendix III). Halted for 1 hour outside Cork. Resumed March at 1.15 p.m. and halted in CORK for 20 minutes 4 Officers and 39 O.R. S.I.H. and 2 Officers, 49 O.R. R.F.A. with 2 guns joined the Column. Marched to Ballincollig where whole column was accommodated in Barracks.	
	[illegible] 16.		4 Officers and 100 O.R. 2/14th entrained at FOTA for BANDON, the remainder of 2/14th being left in FOTA CAMP.	
Ballincollig.	7.5.16.		Marched out of BALLINCOLLIG at 9.0 a.m. and reached at COACHFORD at 1.0 p.m. distance 10 miles. Column encamped on Agricultural Show Ground. Captain Phillips joined the Column as intelligence officer.	
Coachford.	8.5.16.		Marched 9.30 to MACROOM which was reached at 1.0 p.m. Distance 10 miles. Camped in the Castle Park. Brigade Headquarters in the Castle. Sent out 5 detachments at night to search certain houses in the neighbourhood endeavouring to find certain persons wanted by the police, but only one party met with any success, one arrest being made in MACROOM TOWN. Details of these expeditions Appendix IV. News received that remainder of 2/14th had proceeded by train to TRALEE on 7th instant.	
Macroom.	9.5.16		Encamped at MACROOM. Two parties, one consisting of 100 2/15th Bn. and the other of the S.I. Horse and R.F.A. Mounted escort were sent out in search of men wanted by the police. The first party brought back two men and the 2nd were unsuccessful. Reports of Officers Commanding parties Appendix III. Half 2/13th Battalion were detached and sent under Major Thompson to MILLSTREET whereit was desired to make several arrests.	

1577 Wt. W10791/1773 500,000 1/15 D. D. & L. A.D.S.S./Forms/C. 2118.

Instructions regarding War Diaries and Intelligence Summaries are contained in F. S. Regs., Part II. and the Staff Manual respectively. Title pages will be prepared in manuscript.

WAR DIARY
or
INTELLIGENCE SUMMARY.
(Erase heading not required.)

Army Form C. 2118.

Place	Date	Hour	Summary of Events and Information	Remarks and references to Appendices
Macroom.	10.5.16.		Reports receivedthat 2 arrests had been made at MILLSTREET. At 7.30 p.m. a despatch was received from Queenstown by armoured car ordering column to proceed to Millstreet on 11th inst. where the units of 179th Bde. were to entrain for Rosslare. Arrangements had been made to makr more arrests during the night but in view of the march to MILLSTREET the following morning these were cancelled.	
	11.5.16.		A wet morning and the tents has to be struck whilst they were wet. This made the load on the lorries very heavy. The column left MACROOM at 10 a.m. and reached Millstreet at 3.30 where a bivouac was made in a field ½ a mile from the station. News was soon received that the lorries could not get along as tot road would not carry them. Wagons were sent back, but they had sunk so deeply into the roads that they could not move even when relieved of their loads. The 2/15th regiment left in trains leaving at 11 p.m. and 12 midnight. The 2/13th who had a certain numbers of tents which had been brought along by the MILLSTREET detachment, spent the night in them and a barn lent by a farmer and left the following morning by trains leaving at 9.45 and 10.30 a.m. The 2/14th and 2/15th rejoined the Brigade at ROSSLARE. At 7.0 p.m. Brigade Headquarters with 2/14th and 2/15th Battalions and A.S.C. sailed in H.T.CONNAUGHT, the transport sailing in H.T.CYPTER The CONNAUGHT arrived at FISHGUARD at 10.30 p.m. and trains were waiting to convey troops back to SUTTON VENY.	
	12.5.16.		The CYPTER arrived at 3.30 and transport was sent on in 2 trains to SUTTON VENY arriving at 11.30 and 4.0 p.m. Much confusion was caused by the way the transport was disembarked and entrained as both horses and vehicles were off loaded simultaneously from both ends of the ship and just straight into the trains without any sorting being done. The consequence of this was that the horses and wagons were mixed to such an extend that the utmost confusion was caused at the detraining station. A wire was despatched to the Military embarking officer asking for arrangements to be made to prevent a recurrence of this when the transport of the 2/13th and 2/16th were to be disembarked. These two battalions which left ROSSLARE in the same Transports as the remainder of the Brigade arrived 24 hours later and more care being taken in the entraining of the transport the confusion which occurred the previous day was not repeated. The Brigade returned to huts at Longbridge Deverill strength as shown in state (Appendix V).	

1577 Wt. W10791/1773 500,000 1/15 D. D. & L. A.D.S.S./Forms/C. 2118.

Instructions regarding War Diaries and Intelligence Summaries are contained in F. S. Regs., Part II. and the Staff Manual respectively. Title pages will be prepared in manuscript.

WAR DIARY
or
~~INTELLIGENCE SUMMARY.~~
(*Erase heading not required.*)

179th Infy Bde

Army Form C. 2118.

Hour, Date, Place	Summary of Events and Information	Remarks and references to Appendices
14th June Sandhill Camp Longbridge Deverill Wilts	Orders received to Embark at Southampton for Havre on 21st and 22nd June. 2/13th Bn London Regt and 2/14th Bn London Regt on 21st. Bde Headquarters 2/15 and 2/16th Bn London Regiment on 22nd	
15th June	Captain C.M. Phillips and Lieut C.S. Hipwell 2/16th Bn London Regiment proceeded in advance to Havre to act as Landing and entraining officers respectively	
16th June	Closing of all accounts etc	
17th June	Captain Hart, Staff Captain, proceeded in advance to the area of concentration Overseas	
18th June	All correspondence etc prepared for handing over to officer i/c Details	
19th June	Sunday	

Instructions regarding War Diaries and Intelligence Summaries are contained in F. S. Regs., Part II. and the Staff Manual respectively. Title pages will be prepared in manuscript.

WAR DIARY
~~or~~
~~INTELLIGENCE~~ SUMMARY.

(*Erase heading not required.*)

Army Form C. 2118.

Place	Date	Hour	Summary of Events and Information	Remarks and references to Appendices
SANDHILL Camp	20th	June	Final inspection of all ranks Kits Equipment etc	
LONGBRIDGE DEVERILL				
	21st	June	2/13th Bn and 2/14th Bn London Regiment left WARMINSTER. Marching out States	App^x I
	22	June	Bde HdQrs and 2/15th and 2/16th Bns London Regiment left WARMINSTER " " "	"
			Arrived SOUTHAMPTON Docks at 4.30 pm. and embarked on H.T. PANCRAS which sailed for HAVRE at 7.30 pm.	
	23rd	June	Arrived HAVRE at 7.0 am. and disembarked. Bde HdQrs moved to No 2 Camp a distance of about 5 miles. The 2/15th and 2/16th Bns which had also crossed during the night went into a rest camp. The accommodation in the latter was not good the men in many cases having to sleep on bare cobbles. The 2/13th and 2/14th had occupied this camp the previous night and had moved on up country by train during the morning.	
	24th	June	The 2/15th and 2/16th entrained during the day. Bde HdQrs entrained at 6.0 pm. and moved off at 9.0 pm.	
	25th	June	The train was due to arrive at ABBEVILLE at 8.42 am. but owing	

Instructions regarding War Diaries and Intelligence Summaries are contained in F. S. Regs., Part II. and the Staff Manual respectively. Title Pages will be prepared in manuscript.

WAR DIARY
or
INTELLIGENCE SUMMARY
(Erase heading not required.)

Army Form C. 2118

Place	Date	Hour	Summary of Events and Information	Remarks and references to Appendices
25th June	(Con)		to congestion on the line this place was not reached until 2 a.m. Here we were informed that our destination was St Pol where we detrained at 6.30 p.m. and marched to PENIN a distance of 10 miles arriving there at 10.30 p.m. Captain Hart rejoined the brigade here having arranged the billets in this area for the whole brigade and affiliated troops.	
26th June			Bn H.Q. &c remained in billets at PENIN. Information was received that the brigade was to come under the orders of G.O.C. 51st Div and that 2/13th and 2/14th had already moved to ECOIVRES and MAROEUIL to provide working parties to assist the mining being carried out on fronts of 152nd and 153rd Brigades respectively. The 2/15th and 2/16th moved from billets at PENIN and AVERDOINGT to MAROEUIL and ECROIVES respectively.	

Army Form C. 2118

Instructions regarding War Diaries and Intelligence Summaries are contained in F. S. Regs., Part II. and the Staff Manual respectively. Title Pages will be prepared in manuscript.

WAR DIARY
or
INTELLIGENCE SUMMARY
(Erase heading not required.)

Place	Date	Hour	Summary of Events and Information	Remarks and references to Appendices
27th June			Bde Headquarters moved to ECOIVRES. G.O.C. 17th Corps visited new headquarters at 2.30 p.m. accompanied by G.O.C. Div. The Colonels, 2/i in Comd Adjutant and 4 Company comdrs of each battalion were introduced to G.O.C. Corps and a short lecture was delivered by Br. Gen Charles on the line of trenches about to be occupied by 60th Div. 2/13 Bn and 2/14th Bn London Regiment take over mining fatigues from Indian Cavalry.	
28th June			Arrangements made with 153rd Infy Brigade for 2/15th & 2/16th Bns to go into the trenches for instruction. Operation orders for this move were issued by G.O.C. 153rd Inf. Bde.	Op. Order Appendix II
29th June			2/15th and 2/16th Bns London Regt commenced training in the trenches with 153rd Inf. Bde. 2/13th 2/14th Bns carried on with mining fatigues.	
30th June			The O.C. 179th Bde M.G. Coy reported that the Bde M.G. Company had arrived from England and was billeted in the Divisional Area	

1875 Wt. W593/826 1,000,000 4/15 J.B.C. & A. A.D.S.S./Forms/C. 2118.

Army Form C. 2118

Instructions regarding War Diaries and Intelligence Summaries are contained in F. S. Regs., Part II. and the Staff Manual respectively. Title Pages will be prepared in manuscript.

WAR DIARY
or
INTELLIGENCE SUMMARY
(Erase heading not required.)

Place	Date	Hour	Summary of Events and Information	Remarks and references to Appendices
ECOIVRES	30th June		The 2/13th and 2/14th Bns London Regt continue fatigues the 2/15th and 2/16th continue instruction in the trenches with 6th and 7th Bn Black Watch	

1875 Wt. W593/826 1,000,000 4/15 J.B.C. & A. A.D.S.S./Forms/C. 2118.

Appendix I.

179th Infantry Brigade.

MARCHING OUT STATE.

June 1916.

UNIT.	Officers.	Other Ranks.	Horses & Mules.	Vehicles. 4 wheeled.	Vehicles. 2 wheeled.	Bicycles.
Brigade Headquarters.	8.	50.	~~25.~~ 33	7.	-.	14.
2/13th Battn. L.R.	30.	957.	64.	17.	4.	9.
2/14th Battn. L.R.	30.	999.	64.	17.	4.	9.
2/15th Battn. L.R.	31.	1001.	64.	17.	4.	9.
2/16th Battn. L.R.	31.	991.	64.	17.	4.	9.
	130.	3998.	289.	75.	16.	50.

BRIGADIER GENERAL
Comdg. 179th Infantry Brigade.

Appendix 2

Copy No.6.

Operation Order No.110 by Brig-General D.Campbell
Commanding 153rd Infantry Brigade.

28th June, 1916.

1. The 15th and 16th London Regiments will move into the Centre Sector on 29th inst. according to attached table and Table "C.334"
The 15th L.Regiment represent E. Battalion.
" 16th L.Regiment " F. "
" 1/7th Black Watch " A. "
" 1/6th Black Watch " B. "

E. will be attached to A. for training.
F. will be attached to B. for training.

Headquarters: E. at Maison Blanche.
F. at Maison Blanche.

2. Training. Training will be carried out as follows:-

Right Half Battalion:

Individual Training 29th-30th June.	Half the Officers and N.C.Os. of each Company in alternate reliefs of 6 hours so as to include night and day work. To commence at 6 p.m. 29th instant. 1st Relief 6 p.m. to 12 midnight. 2nd Relief 12 midnight to 6 a.m. 1st Relief 6 a.m. to 12 noon. 2nd Relief 12 noon to 6 p.m.
Platoon Training - 30th - 1st July.	Platoons in Support move up to Observation and Firing Lines.
Company Training - 1st - 2nd July.	Companies in support move up to Observation and Firing Lines.

Left Half Battalion.

2nd - 3rd July.	as above.
3rd - 4th July.	as above.
4th - 5th July.	as above.

Individual. Officers and N.C.O's receiving training will as far as possible be attached to Platoons of A. and B. Battalions holding the same section of Firing Line as their Platoon will occupy on the following night - and will be attached to opposite numbers.

Platoon. During Platoon Training 1 Officer and 1 N.C.O. of A. and B. Battalions will be attached to the Platoon under instruction.

Company. 1 Officer and 4 N.C.O's of A. and B. Battalions will be attached to Companies of E. and F. Battalions.

3. Relief. the 1/5th Gordon Highlanders and 1 Company of 1/7th Gordon Highlanders in Elbe and Rhine Shelters will be relieved (less the undermentioned details) on arrival of E. and F. and on relief will move to billets at MAROEUIL.
Details. Remaining. The Officer Commanding 1/5th Gordon Highlanders (1 Coy.) will detail 1 Officers 4 N.C.O's and 8 men per Company of E. and F. taking over to give instruction in carrying of meals, stores, T.M.Ammunition, water, working of Railways, etc. and to act as Guides, while in Support and Reserve, also instruction as to reinforcing front line from Supports.

4. Lewis Guns. Two Guns of E. and two of F. Battalions will relieve four Guns of 1/5th Gordon Highlanders in Support and thereafter will be under O.Cs. A. and B. for positions and instruction - (E. and F. are armed with only 4 Guns per Battalion). This relief to be completed by 11 a.m. 29th - on relief 4 Guns of 1/5th Gordon Highlanders to MAROEUIL. One N.C.O. or intelligent

Lewis Gunner to remain attached to each Gun Team to instruct until absorbed into Firing Line when A. and B. Battalions will provide the Instructor.

5. Signal Sections. Signal Sections of 1/5th Gordon Highlanders and 1/7th Gordon Highlanders will remain in Trenches in charge of the System. E. and F. Battalions will attach for training
1 Operator per Company.
2 " " Headquarters.
Period of Training 2 days.

6. Guides. The 1/7th Gordon Highlanders at MAROEUIL will provide Guides.
1 per half Platoon.
1 from each Sector Lewis Guns.
who will conduct parties as follows:-
E. Battalion Platoons and Lewis Guns to Junction of Sapper and MAISON BLANCHE.
F. Battalion Platoons and Lewis Guns to junction of ~~Sapper~~ Territorial with BETHUNE ROAD (4 Platoons MAISON BLANCHE).

At the above Junctions the 1/7th Gordon Highlanders Guides will hand over to Guides detailed by 1/5th Gordon Highlanders and Coy. of 1/7th Gordon Highlanders who will conduct to their respective positions.

The Platoons of E. and F. should each be numbered from 1 to 16 and should arrive in that order.

Guides should be provided with cards having their Platoon numbers E. 5. F. 12. so as to ensure the 1/5th Gordon Highlanders Guides getting the proper parties.

7. Trench Stores. The Officers of the 153rd Infantry Brigade attached to Companies of E. and F. Battalions in Support and Reserve will be responsible for Trench Stores until further notice.

8. Reports. Progress of reliefs to be sent to Adv. Brigade Headquarters Corn and MAISON BLANCHE.

(sd) J. MILNE.
Captain,
A/Brigade Major, 153rd Infantry Brigade.

Issued at 2.30 p.m.
Copy No. 1 retained.
" 2 O.C., 1/6th Black Watch.
" 3 O.C., 1/7th Black Watch.
" 4. O.C., 1/5th Gordon Highlanders.
" 5. O.C., 1/7th Gordon Highlanders.
" 6. Headquarters, 179th Infantry Brigade.
" 7. Staff Captain, 153rd Infantry Brigade.
" 8. 153rd Company Machine Gun Corps.
" 9. Headquarters, 51st (High.) Division.

MOVEMENT TABLE.

UNIT.	LEAVE BILLETS.	ROUTE.	DESTINATION.	REMARKS.
2 Coy. 15/L.Regt.	3 p.m.	BRAY MAROEUIL. Territorial Avenue. Bethune Road Trench. Sapper Avenue.	MAISON BLANCHE for Support Line. R. Sub-Sector.	Attached 1/7th Black Watch.
1 Coy. 15/L.Regt.	3.20 p.m.	-do-	MAISON BLANCHE for Reserve R. Sub-Sector.	-do-
1 Coy. 16/L.Regt.	3.40 p.m.	Via MAROEUIL. Territorial Avenue. GUILLERMOT Avenue.	Elbe for Support. Line L. Sub-sector.	Attached 1/6th Black Watch.
1 Coy. 16/L.Regt.	4 p.m.	-do-	Elbe for Vistula for Reserve L.Sub-sector.	-do-
1 Coy. 16/L.Regt.	4.20 p.m.	-do-	Rhine and Elbe.	Brigade Reserve.
1 Coy. 15/L.Regt.	4.40 p.m.	MAROEUIL Territorial Avenue, Bethune Road Trench. Sapper Avenue.	MAISON BLANCHE for Fork Redoubt Shelters.	-do-
1 Coy. 16/L.Regt.	5 p.m.	-do-	MAISON BLANCHE.	-do-

Parties moving East of Brunehaut Farm will move in ½ Platoons at 300x interval.

600

VOL. II

Vol 2

CONFIDENTIAL

WAR DIARY

179th INFANTRY BRIGADE
HEADQUARTERS

JULY 1st 1916 - JULY 31st 1916

D. A. G.,
3rd Echelon,
Base.

Herewith War Diary for 179th Infantry Brigade from 1st day of Mobilization to 30th June 1916.

Brigade Headquarters.
July 1st 1916.

BRIGADIER GENERAL,
Comdg. 179th Infantry Brigade.

Instructions regarding War Diaries and Intelligence Summaries are contained in F. S. Regs., Part II. and the Staff Manual respectively. Title Pages will be prepared in manuscript.

WAR DIARY or ~~INTELLIGENCE SUMMARY~~

(Erase heading not required.)

179th Infantry Brigade

VOL. 2

Army Form C. 2118.

Place	Date	Hour	Summary of Events and Information	Remarks and references to Appendices
ECOIVRES	July 1st	–	Brigade Headquarters remained in Chateaux at ECOIVRES. The G.O.C. Brigade and Brigade Major visited the line of trenches in which 2/15th and 2/16th were under instruction. Owing to extensive mining operations on both sides the original front line of trench had ceased to exist except in the form of sap heads which in a zig-zag ran out to the near lip of a mine crater and were used as observation posts by a few bombers. At an average distance of 50 yards behind this line of posts a fire trench had been constructed. This was in very bad condition with the exception of the dugouts which were deep and good.	[illegible]
	2nd		A small raid was made on night of 1st/2nd by the Germans into the trenches in which the 2/13th Bn were doing mining fatigues, inflicting several casualties on one of the working parties. Two thousand Steel helmets arrived for 2/13th and 2/14th. 500 of these were handed to 2/15th & 2/16th.	[illegible]
	3rd		Brigadier and Bde Major again visited trenches which 2/16th and 2/15th were being instructed in, this line being the line which the Brigade is eventually to take over.	[illegible]

1875 Wt. W593/826 1,000,000 4/15 J.B.C. & A. A.D.S.S./Forms/C. 2118.

Instructions regarding War Diaries and Intelligence Summaries are contained in F. S. Regs., Part II. and the Staff Manual respectively. Title Pages will be prepared in manuscript.

WAR DIARY
or
INTELLIGENCE SUMMARY
(Erase heading not required.)

Army Form C. 2118.

Place	Date	Hour	Summary of Events and Information	Remarks and references to Appendices
ECOIVRES	July 4		A detachment of 4 Officers and 56 O.R. which had been attending a course at a Trench Mortar School returned to Bn H.Q. fully equipped with Stokes guns. This party now forms 179th Light Trench Mortar battery under 2Lieut W Anderson 2/14th Bn L.R.	W.A.H.
"	5th		2/15th 2/16th Bns completed their tour of instruction in the trenches and took over the evening fatigues from 2/13th and 2/14th Bns these battalions returning to billets in ECOIVRES and MAROEUIL	W.A.H.
"	6th		The medium Trench Mortar Battery No 60.X. arrived at ECOIVRES to be attached for tactical purposes to the brigade commanded by	W.A.H.
"	7th		The personnel of Medium Trench Mortar Battery proceeded to be attached to the Medium T.M.B. of 153rd Inf: Bde for instruction.	W.A.H.
"	8th		Nothing to record	W.A.H.
"	9th		Nothing to record	W.A.H.
"	10th		Nothing to record	W.A.H.

1875 Wt. W593/826 1,000,000 4/15 J.B.C. & A. A.D.S.S./Forms/C. 2118.

Instructions regarding War Diaries and Intelligence Summaries are contained in F. S. Regs., Part II. and the Staff Manual respectively. Title Pages will be prepared in manuscript.

WAR DIARY
or
INTELLIGENCE SUMMARY
(Erase heading not required.)

Army Form C. 2118.

Place	Date	Hour	Summary of Events and Information	Remarks and references to Appendices
ECOIVRES	July 11th		Operation orders issued for the relief of 13th Bn. R. Innis. Fus. by the 119th Infy Bde in centre sector M2 to O1.	[illegible]
			The defences of this sector consist of:-	
			(a) A line of observation held by sentry groups found by companies garrisoning the line of Resistance and posted in part of the old French line. In the neighbourhood of mine craters and where the enemy's lines approach within bombing distance, sentry groups are replaced by bombing parties who find their own sentries and form part of the line of observation	
			(b) A line of Resistance. This is the main position and is to be held on to till the last	
			(c) A support line which includes 3 strong posts. These posts are not occupied as they show up clearly on aeroplane photographs and are subjected to heavy bombardment both from guns and mortars	
			(d) A third line along a sunken road which contains two strong posts both of which suffer from the same disadvantage as the strong posts in the support	

1875 Wt. W593/826 1,000,000 4/15 J.B.C. & A. A.D.S.S./Forms/C. 2118.

Instructions regarding War Diaries and Intelligence Summaries are contained in F. S. Regs., Part II. and the Staff Manual respectively. Title Pages will be prepared in manuscript.

WAR DIARY
or
INTELLIGENCE SUMMARY
(Erase heading not required.)

Army Form C. 2118.

Place	Date	Hour	Summary of Events and Information	Remarks and references to Appendices
ECOIVRES	11th		line except that they are not subjected to mortar fire.	
			In view of the above is the fortified work of MAISON BLANCHE which with the fortified village of NEUVILLE St VAAST on the left and ECURIE on the right command the valleys known as FOND de VASE and PROFOND VAL.	
			The front line trenches were on the whole in very bad repair and in many places almost ceased to exist. The communication trenches are good and boarded in almost every instance.	
			The support trenches and strong posts have suffered considerably from the weather as the garrisons are not sufficient to keep them in repair.	Shk
	12th		Relief commenced 2/12th Bn Trench Mortars and Machine Guns taking over their positions in the line. The moves on this day were carried out according to programme and without casualties.	Shk
	13th		Half of 2/11th Bn not already in the line for instruction moved up the O.C. 2/14th taking over command of the right subsector	

Instructions regarding War Diaries and Intelligence Summaries are contained in F. S. Regs., Part II. and the Staff Manual respectively. Title Pages will be prepared in manuscript.

WAR DIARY
or
INTELLIGENCE SUMMARY
(Erase heading not required.)

Army Form C. 2118.

Place	Date	Hour	Summary of Events and Information	Remarks and references to Appendices
Trenches E. of NUEVILLE ST VAAST	13th		(Con) 5/6th Bn moved from finding fatigue parties at [illegible] and ANZIN to support line	
			2/15th Bn moved from finding fatigue duties at NEUVILLE ST VAAST to Divisional Reserve at BRAY HUTS	
			All the movements were carried out according to programme	
			The G.O.C. 183rd Brigade with staff assumed Advanced Brigade Head quarters at 12 midnight 13th/14th. G.O.C. 179th Infy Bde taking over command of the sector	
	14th		A certain amount of activity with stay[?] bombs and [illegible] on both sides. Our artillery firing in occasionally silencing the enemy mortars	
			The enemy were heard tamping. One of our mines which was ready loaded was tamped up and blown and it is believed that the enemy gallery was seriously damaged. The crater was thrown up.	
	15th		French mortars were active at intervals during the day. The German mortar what is known as an "Oil Can" [illegible]	

WAR DIARY
or
INTELLIGENCE SUMMARY
(Erase heading not required.)

Army Form C. 2118

Instructions regarding War Diaries and Intelligence Summaries are contained in F. S. Regs., Part II. and the Staff Manual respectively. Title Pages will be prepared in manuscript.

Place	Date	Hour	Summary of Events and Information	Remarks and references to Appendices
Trenches	15th		A rough form of bomb cylindrical in shape hence its name. It is filled with high explosive and is fired off some wooden arrangement which is buried in the ground. It is a very destructive weapon against trenches.	
			At 2.0 pm the 2/15th Batt moved up to relieve 2/14th which battalion on being relieved went into the support. The 2/16th Bn relieved 2/13th Bn in left subsection the 2/13th going to reserve in BRAY HUTS	[illegible]
	16th		Our medium T.M. Battery exploded an ammunition or bomb store in the enemy lines. All working parties from 58th Division were ordered to join their units. This hindered the mining operations considerably as the sandbags which were filled from the tunnels could not be carried away and distributed the trenches near the mine shafts becoming blocked with them. The enemy were active at intervals with Trench Mortars.	[illegible]
	17th		Quiet on the whole during the day. Trench mortars were active at night and retaliation was called for from the artillery. The	

1875 Wt. W593/826 1,000,000 4/15 J.B.C. & A. A.D.S.S./Forms/C. 2118.

Instructions regarding War Diaries and Intelligence Summaries are contained in F. S. Regs., Part II. and the Staff Manual respectively. Title Pages will be prepared in manuscript.

WAR DIARY
or
INTELLIGENCE SUMMARY
(Erase heading not required.)

Army Form C. 2118.

Place	Date	Hour	Summary of Events and Information	Remarks and references to Appendices
[illegible]	17th		The enemy snipers were soon silenced.	
	18th		Enemy seems to be keenly alert for any movement in our lines and is quick to fire with T.Ms. and rifle grenades if any movement be noticed. There have been heard motors about near the front line enemy trenches and it is thought that he moves his T.Ms about in this manner.	[illegible]
	19th		The 11th Siege Battery registered on trenches opposite our right centre companies. This appears to have had the effect of keeping the enemy T.Ms very quiet as they scarcely fired at all during the latter part of the day. As a rule they are most active between 4.0 pm and 7.0 pm. Reliefs were carried out battalions going into same positions in firing line as they were in prior to last relief. The battalion relieved in the firing line going back into support and reserve in the opposite order to which they were before. The relief was carried out quickly and with only 2 casualties.	[illegible]

1375 Wt. W593/826 1,000,000 4/15 J.B.C. & A. A.D.S.S./Forms/C. 2118.

Instructions regarding War Diaries and Intelligence Summaries are contained in F. S. Regs., Part II. and the Staff Manual respectively. Title Pages will be prepared in manuscript.

WAR DIARY
or
INTELLIGENCE SUMMARY
(Erase heading not required.)

Army Form C. 21

Place	Date	Hour	Summary of Events and Information	Remarks and references to Appendices
Trenches	20	-	Our trenches having been badly damaged by hostile ~~Artillery~~ Trench Mortar fire Our Trench Mortars in conjunction with Divl Artillery group and 11th Siege battery concentrated on a portion of the enemy's line between A16 D 9.4 and A16 a 9½ - 8½. The bombardment lasted 40 minutes and appeared to have the desired effect as the enemy Trench Mortars which were usually active in the evening did not fire another round all day. While the bombardment was being carried out the men were withdrawn from the Sap heads so that the 18 pdrs might fire with safety on the German front line. The evacuation and reoccupying of these Saps was carried out without casualties.	D.A.
Trenches	21		A quiet day on the whole. Enemy guns active in the morning searching for our gun positions. Their Trench Mortars fired intermittently throughout the day.	D.A.
	22		Trench Mortar activity on both sides. Our artillery firing salvos at 2 places where Trench Mortars where supposed to be. No definite results however were obtained.	D.A.

1375 Wt. W593/826 1,000,000 4/15 J.B.C. & A. A.D.S.S./Forms/C. 2118.

Instructions regarding War Diaries and Intelligence Summaries are contained in F. S. Regs., Part II. and the Staff Manual respectively. Title Pages will be prepared in manuscript.

WAR DIARY
or
INTELLIGENCE SUMMARY
(Erase heading not required.)

Army Form C. [illegible]8

Place	Date	Hour	Summary of Events and Information	Remarks and references to Appendices
TRENCHES	23rd		Enemy trench mortars were active between 12.30 and 1.0 pm. At 4.10 pm Enemy opened a brisk fire employing artillery oil cans sling bombs and rifle grenades on our front line. This was apparently in retaliation for a bombardment of the enemy trenches organised by 101st Brigade	[illegible]
	24th		The enemy fired a number of aerial torpedoes late in the afternoon apart from this nothing of note occurred. It is thought that this is their day for relief.	[illegible]
	25th		An abnormally quiet day. A patrol of two men went out at 10.0 pm and returned at 9.0 am. They passed close to two listening posts and four enemy Trench Mortars. They reported that the enemy line appeared to be very lightly held.	[illegible]
	26th		Another very quiet day. In the early hours of the morning Enemy blew a mine opposite left sector but no attack was delivered	[illegible]
	27th		Relief of battalions in the firing line commenced at 8.0 am and was completed without casualty by 1.45 pm. The enemy were	

1875 Wt. W593/826 1,000,000 4/15 J.B.C. & A. A.D.S.S./Forms/C. 2118.

Instructions regarding War Diaries and Intelligence Summaries are contained in F. S. Regs., Part II. and the Staff Manual respectively. Title Pages will be prepared in manuscript.

WAR DIARY
or
INTELLIGENCE SUMMARY
(Erase heading not required.)

Army Form C. 2118

Place	Date	Hour	Summary of Events and Information	Remarks and references to Appendices
Trenches	27th	(Con)	quiet all day and made no reply to our Trench mortars	WAA
"	28th		There was a little more activity on the part of the enemy who appeared to be registering as though new gunners had come into the line opposite. The enemy Trench Mortars were active in the evening on the left subsector.	WAA
"	29th		At 4.30 am. 2 German Soldiers of 184 Regiment surrendered to a post of 2/15th Rt London Regiment. At 5.0 pm. our Trench mortars in conjunction with the Corps Heavy Artillery and the Divisional Artillery bombarded the enemy trenches behind the Argyl Crater for 20 minutes. There was very little retaliation and much damage appeared to be done to the enemy's support trenches. One of the enemy's 6" guns from a new position on the VIMY Ridge fired about 20 rounds which mostly fell in the next brigade area on our left.	WAA
	30th		Trench mortars were active in the morning on our left, otherwise a quiet day	WAA
	31st		A very quiet day nothing to record	WAA

Army Form C. 2[illegible]8

Instructions regarding War Diaries and Intelligence Summaries are contained in F. S. Regs., Part II. and the Staff Manual respectively. Title Pages will be prepared in manuscript.

WAR DIARY
or
INTELLIGENCE SUMMARY
(Erase heading not required.)

Place	Date	Hour	Summary of Events and Information	Remarks and references to Appendices
			July 1916 — List of Appendices	
			Appendix III — Casualties for month of July	
			" IV — Strength states of units on 1st and 31st July	
			" V — Daily Intelligence Summaries 13 – 31st July.	
			[illegible]	

1875 Wt. W593/826 1,000,000 4/15 J.B.C. & A. A.D.S.S./Forms/C. 2118.

Appendix III

179th Infantry Brigade.

CASUALTIES FOR THE MONTH OF JULY, 1916.

UNIT.	KILLED.	WOUNDED.	TOTAL.
2/13th Battalion London Regiment.	11.	31.	42.
2/14th " " "	10.	x28.	38.
2/15th " " "	10.	32.	42.
2/16th " " "	6.	26.	32.
179th Machine Gun Co.	1.	x2.	3.
179th Light Trench Mortar Battery.	-	1.	1.
60xMedium " " "	1.	-	1.
	39.	120.	159.

xIncludes 1 Accidental.

N.B. This does not include the Officers casualties shewn below.

OFFICERS, KILLED.

2/14th Battalion London Regiment:- 2/Lieut. A.C. Wilson.

2/Lieut. A.T. Powell, (Camerons) attached.

OFFICERS, WOUNDED.

2/14th Battalion London Regiment:- 2/Lieut. A. Chisholm.

2/Lieut. W.J. Bethune, (Camerons) attached.

2/16th Battalion London Regiment:- 2/Lieut. L.L. Falck.

Appendix IV

STRENGTH RETURN.

As at JULY 1st 1916.

UNIT.	OFFICERS.	OTHER RANKS.
179th Infantry Brigade Headquarters	11.	49.
2/13th Battalion London Regiment.	30.	983.
2/14th Battalion London Regiment.	29.	983.
2/15th Battalion London Regiment.	30.	965.
2/16th Battalion London Regiment.	31.	972.
179th Machine Gun Co.	10.	142.
179th Light Trench Mortar Battery	4.	46.
60x Medium Trench Mortar Battery.	2.	23.
	147.	4,183.

STRENGTH RETURN.

As at 31st July, 1916.

UNIT.	OFFICERS.	OTHER RANKS.
179th Infantry Brigade Headquarters.	12.	49.
2/13th Battalion London Regiment.	30.	926.
2/14th Battalion London Regiment.	38.	948.
2/15th Battalion London Regiment.	32.	944.
2/16th Battalion London Regiment.	31.	964.
179th Machine Gun Co.	10.	141.
179th Light Trench Mortar Battery.	4.	46.
60x Medium Trench Mortar Battery.	1.	23.
	158.	4,041.

This Return includes Officers, N.C.Os. and other Ranks attached from other Units.

CONFIDENTIAL.

179th Infantry Brigade,

DAILY INTELLIGENCE SUMMARY - 10 a.m. 13/7/16 to 10 a.m. 14/7/16.

CENTRE SECTOR.

No. 1 SUB-SECTOR:

1. SITUATION: Normal. The enemy have been fairly active with Trench Mortars during the last 24 hours. They exploded a Mine last evening.

2. TRENCH MORTARS. Enemy Trench Mortars were active from 10 a.m. till noon yesterday and again during the afternoon. Aerial Torpedoes, Oilcans and Sling Bombs were mostly used and were chiefly directed on point where BENTATA joins the Firing Line and at Junction of DOUAI and FIRING LINE. Considerable damage was done to the Trenches at both these points. Our Lewis Gun Officer reports that he had to move No. 3 Gun Position from Point K in consequence. It is thought the Enemy T.Ms. are intended for Mine Sap Head just behind Point K. During the night the Enemy were again active with T.Ms. chiefly on the front and support lines of the Right Centre Co. Considerable damage to Trenches was done.

3. MINES. The Enemy blew up a Mine to the RIGHT of M.2 at 7.10 p.m. No damage was done to our Trenches. The Mine was some distance on our right front and was not occupied by the Enemy. Our Artillery heavily bombarded this part of the Enemy Lines from 7.15 p.m. till 7.45 p.m. and must have caused considerable damage to the Enemy's Earthworks. The Enemy replied to this bombardment with T.Ms. directed on our front line of the Right and Right Centre Co's.

4. ARTILLERY. Our Artillery heavily shelled Enemy Front Line at 7.15 p.m. opposite the Right of M.2. At 10 p.m. last night our Guns opened heavy fire on the Enemy front left of our left Co. Enemy retaliated on our line with T.Ms.

5. MACHINE GUNS. Enemy swept our parapet with Machine Gun Fire at intervals during the night.

6. SNIPING. Our Snipers observed throughout the day but were not able to secure a favourable target. Two or three of the Enemy were seen but disappeared again instantly. Two shots were fired at periscopes which were at once removed.

7. AIRCRAFT. No Enemy Aircraft were observed over this Sector.

8. INFORMATION. Pieces of Enemy Aerial Torpedoes were picked up yesterday all dated 31st May 1916. The Enemy appeared to be working in his Trench during the afternoon. Parties of 2 or 3 of the Enemy have been seen and heard in the SAP leading into the EASTERN lip of the CLAUDOT Crater. Their uniform was of BLUE-GREY and they were wearing flat round grey caps with black bands. Our T.Ms. dropped 5 shells into the Sap. Further activity has however been observed.

WORK REPORT (Done).

Right Co. Wired Sap 35a. with gooseberries.
Drained and cleared Fire Trench.
Drained & cleared & rivetted RAWSON St. Built new Fire Step.

Right Centre Co. Sap 35 b. Blocking with chevaux de frise and wire entanglements. Fire Trench. Deppening & preparing for Trench Boards. Filling Sandbags and clearing way where Trench has been blown in.

Left Centre Co. Carrying Sandbags from BORLES to DOUBLEMONT.
Repairing parapet in DOUBLEMONT between BERENS and BORLES.
Cleaning Trench between BORLES and DOUAI after bombardment.

Left Co: Wiring Gooseberries.
Clearing Trench and filling Sandbags between MERPILLAT and CLAUDOT.
-do- -do- FROGER & CLAUDOT.
Clearing MERPILLAT SAP.
Clearing Fire Bay left of MERPILLAT.
Clearing left arm of MERPILLAT.
Filling Sandbags 2nd Bay left of Claudot.
Repairing 2nd fire Bay to right of CLAUDOT.
Making Gooseberries.
Repairing Fire Bay to right of CLAUDOT.

WORK PROPOSED.

Right Co. Continue revetting in RAWSON ST.
Re-lay Trench Boards and dig sump holes.
Wire top left side of SAP 35a.

Right Centre Co. Repairing Fire Trench.
Blocking Sap 35a.
Making Entanglements.

Left Centre Co. Clean DOUBLEMONT - repair and reset Trench Boards.
Rebuild parapet between DOUAI and BIRAS.

Left Co. Strengthening wire in front of observation line between FROGER and MERPILLAT.
Opening left arm of MERPILLAT, deepening and revetting fire Trench between MERPILLAT and CLAUDOT. Improving parapet and parados of Fire Trench.

CENTRE SECTOR.

No. 2. SUB-SECTOR.

1. OPERATIONS. (a) Ours:
RAID by Rear Party of 5th Gordons assisted by 153rd Battery T.M. Light, 1/51st Battery Medium T.M. and Artillery, on German Lines.
(b) Hostile: Nothing to report.

2. INTELLIGENCE: (a) Aircraft.) Nothing to report.
(b) Balloons.)
(c) Flares. The night being moderately light the Enemy used less than usual except during our raid.
(d) SIGNALS: Nothing to report.
(e) WIRE: The Enemy was well cut by our T.M.Batteries for the Raiding Party.
(f) WIND: The wind during 24 hours was mild to light breezes - chiefly between W. and S.W.

3. GENERAL. (1) ARTILLERY.
(a) OURS: Our Artillery was not very active during the early part of the day. A slow duel took place between 12 noon and 1 p.m. The enemy lines were shelled between 7.30 and 7.50 p.m. and the guns continued intermittently until 8 p.m.
To assist Raiding Party - Artillery Bombarded Enemy Lines at 9.57 p.m. lifted at 10.15 p.m. and ceased fire at 10.25 p.m.
Bursts of fire were delivered at 11.20 and 11.50 p.m.
Raiding party reported our shells falling short.

(b) ENEMY: Not active. About 20 "whizz-bangs" were sent over between 1.50 p.m. and 2.30 p.m. Bursts occurred about 100 yards behind our Front Line. Centre Co. doing no material harm.
A few rounds were fired at the MILL at 7.40 p.m.
In reply to our bombardment Enemy opened Fire at about 10.5 p.m. and sent over about 20 "WHIZZ-BANGS" in direction of MAITLAND ST. No material damage. GRANDE BRETELLE and PHILLIP reported as badly hit. (B. Co.)

(2) T.M.
(a) OURS: 1/51 T.M.B.
Fired at 9.57 p.m. to cut Enemy wire and knock out suspected M.G.Emplacements. Wire was cut and Raiding party was not met by M.G. Fire.
1/53rd T.M.B.
Fired to assist R

aiding

1/53rd T.M.B.
Fired to assist raiding party. Objective: Salient in German Line Pts. 444 and 455.
(b) ENEMY: Not active.

(3) M.Gs.
(a) OURS: Assisted in raid at 10 p.m. Fired about 2,300 rounds.
(b) ENEMY: Nothing to report.

(4) BOMBS: Nothing to report beyond raid.
(5) SNIPERS: No hits claimed.
Good post decided upon - construction to be carried on tonight.
(6) ENEMY ATTITUDE. Quiet generally, heard talking in their Sap at 11.15 p.m. from CRATER 810.

4. WORK: (a) OURS:
All available men (B.Co.) were employed widening and clearing GRANDE BRETELLE and PHILLIP at 12 midnight. Working party started repairing damage and clearing out above two Trenches after Enemy retaliation for raid. 6 men and 1 N.C.O. assisted R.Es to open up Mine Shaft L. which had been filled up by a shell.

(b) ENEMY:
Cpl. Way of M.G.Section reports Enemy throwing up Earth 80 yds. in front of our line - L.G.D.Position - 8.30 p.m.
Due E. of Junction of GUILLERMOT AVENUE and EDINBURGH ST. Enemy was working in his lines (Reported to L.G. and T.M.).

MINING:
Sentries: Right (b) Co. report noises. Mining Officers have been informed.
Post at head of PHILIP (808) was drawn in 40 yards at 1 a.m. on Mining Officers received through HORSE.

(sd) E.W.BAIRD.
BRIGADIER GENERAL,
Comdg. 179th Infantry Brigade.

HORSE.
July 14th 1916.

I.R.2.

CONFIDENTIAL.

179th Infantry Brigade.

DAILY INTELLIGENCE SUMMARY - 8 a.m. 14/7/1916 to 8 a.m. 15/7/1916.

1. OPERATIONS.
Ours. Nothing to report.
Enemy. Enemy T.M. quiet throughout morning and early afternoon. At 4 p.m. very active with xSling Bombs, Oilcans, Aerial Torpedoes, chiefly directed on M.2. Retaliation effected with a few 18 pr. shells. Again at 7.30 to 8.20 p.m. Enemy active. Retaliation by Howitzers and Stoke Guns. Between 9 and 10 p.m. Enemy T.Ms. active.
Artillery shelled the DOUAI Trench near Junction with ELBE but no damage done.
Enemy active again at 1.30 a.m. T.Ms. Our Artillery retaliated on N.1. and M.2. about 1.45 a.m. when Enemy fire ceased.
MINES. As Enemy was heard tamping - N.40 R.Shaft was tamped up and blown at 3.30 p.m. Enemy did not retaliate.
MACHINE GUNS. The following points were searched with Indirect Fire from 9.30 to 10.30 p.m.:-
Trenches near A.11a. 1 - 6.
Road near A.17a. 5 - 2.
Cross Roads on LES TILLEULS at A.11a. 9 - 9.
Suspected Enemy Headquarters at A.17d. 1½ - 6.

2. INTELLIGENCE. Stokes Gun in STAFFORD ST. fired 11 rounds at Snipers Post E. of PULPIT and Enemy Sniper has not been active since.
Lewis Guns fired at Enemy Working Parties as follows:-
10.10 p.m. on Enemy Working Party left of PULPIT and party dispersed.
10.35 p.m. fired on Working Party 40 yards N. of PULPIT.
2.35 a.m. Lewis Gun dispersed a Working Party on far lip of Crater 805.
AIRCRAFT. At 4.30 a.m. one of our Aeroplanes passed over; was heavily fired upon but not hit.

3. GENERAL. Enemy working parties appear very bold.
Two of the Enemy were observed opposite VISSEC SAP. One appeared to be a youth wearing a hard round cap similar to the British Cap but of Blue Grey Colour with black facings. After the Mine was blown, a whistle was heard which is believed to be an Enemy Signal for Ambulance.
Trucks were heard moving in the Enemy Line opposite CLAUDOT

4. WORK DONE. Ours. Repairing and clearing Firing Line, repairing GRANDE BRETELLE and PHILLIP.
Widening near M.H. and Ammunition recess built at N.O.C. parapet strengthened near N.A.

(sd) E.W.BAIRD.
BRIGADIER GENERAL
Comdg 179th Infantry Brigade.

July 15th 1916.

CONFIDENTIAL.

179th Infantry Brigade.

DAILY INTELLIGENCE SUMMARY. 10 a.m. 15/7/16 to 10 a.m. 16/7/16.

1. OPERATIONS.

Ours. The following localities were searched with indirect M.G.Fire between 10 p.m. and 11 p.m. last night from
N.O.D. Position (a) Trenches near A.5. 3 - 4.
(b) LES TILLEULS Road from A.17a. 6 - 2 and A.11a. 6 - 9.
N.O.C. Position (a) Road near A.17.
(b) Cross Roads in LES TILLEULS.

Retaliation by our T.Ms. about 10 p.m. took place about 30 rounds being sent over and Enemy fire ceased. Damage to Trench at Junction of CLAUDOT - BENTATA was severe. and telephone lines shattered. Observation Line near FROGER had a bad hit necessitating 15' of frontage being repaired with Sand-bags. Lewis Gun at No.6 was active in covering working party repairing parapet

Enemy. About 11 a.m. the Enemy shelled FORK REDOUBT with 4.2. H.E.Shrapnel. Slight damage caused to parapet. Enemy Artillery was active throughout the evening until about 10.30 p.m. and was directed on line extending from VICTOIRE BENTATA. Sniping was active, particularly at stand-to.

2. INTELLIGENCE. At 2.45 a.m. Enemy put up an orange coloured flame; this was followed at 2.50 a.m. by 2 rounds from a Trench Mortar on front line, at bottom of LICHFIELD STREET. Enemy Working party seen opposite PULPIT about 1 a.m. was dispersed by STOKES GUN Fire.

About 4.15 a.m. a figure in a long brown Overcoat appeared on German Parapet for a few seconds opposite BENTATA. Observer could not determine if he were an Officer - but his object appeared to be to examine the result of the Trench Mortar Fire.

At 11.30 p.m. an Aeroplane flying low passed over Brigade Headquarters but identity could not be seen. From the sound of the Exhaust it appeared to be flying towards the Enemy Eastwards.

3. GENERAL. From about 10.30 p.m. onwards the night passed quietly on both sides.

4. WORK DONE. Observation Trench parapets strengthened where required. Wire strengthened between CLAUDOT and FROGER and in front of MERPILLAT and VISSEC. Draining of Trenches near ZIVY Redoubt and revetting. Overhead cover Gun No.02 position repaired. Refuse pit started near W.S.D. H.S.A. Emplacement improved.

(sd) W.H.HERBERT.
Major,
BRIGADE MAJOR,
179th Infantry Brigade.

CONFIDENTIAL. I.R.4.

DAILY INTELLIGENCE REPORT.

(From 10 a.m. 16/7/1916 to 10 a.m. 17/7/1916)

OPERATIONS: (a) Our Medium T.M.B. from No.3 Gun when firing at Point 18 appeared to penetrate an Ammunition or Bomb Store as a severe explosion was observed, sparks and timber flying in all directions. No. 1 Gun fired 7 rounds on Points B.1, 2, 4, 5 and 6, also five rounds in retaliation of T.M.Fire at point B.10. Points J.10, 11 & 12 and P.10 - 2 - 3 - 4 were also fired at. M. Gun fired between 9.45 and 10.15 p.m. indirect:-

N.O.D. Gun at A.10b. 8.8....... 500 rounds.
" " " A.17a. 2.7....... 250 rounds.
N.O.C. " " A.11a. 1.6....... 500 rounds.
" " " A.17d. 1½.6...... 250 rounds.

(b) Two distinct phases in activity. The first from 12 to 2 p.m. desultory firing on N.1 and heavy shelling about 50 mostly H.E.4.2. on to right of M.2, the shells apparently coming from direction of VIMY.

The second phase commenced at 12.10 a.m. After noticeable cessation of Very Lights a Bombardment was suddenly opened. Retaliation was called for and obtained with much success. The enemy shelling was from a point 100° from Saphead 34a.

INTELLIGENCE. During the Enemy Bombardment from 12.20 a.m. and at intervals of about ten minutes, the Enemy put up a single red rocket. Working party on lip of Crater 277 and fired at by Lewis Gun. An Enemy Sniper post is suspected in the shallow crater due South of 277 Crater and is under close observation.

A Snipers post has been located opposite point 765 and a bearing will be taken.

An Aeroplance (ours) passed over N.1.at 10.30 a.m.

A number of our shells were observed to fall short of our Observation Line and it is estimated that nearly one-third failed to explode. When Enemy Oil-Cans came over a very bright flare was simultaneously put up and it is suggested this is a trick to prevent our seeing the Oil-Can in the air.

Enemy M.G.Emplacement located at SHEBAS BREAST and pointed out to Artillery.

GENERAL. No patrolling took place and no sniper hits recorded.

WORK DONE. Repairing Trench near M.H. damaged by bombardment on Saturday night. M.G.Emplacement improved at N.S.B. Refuse pit dug at O.3. Arc Mountain placed in N.C.A.

Removing Sandbags from Miners Dumps and depositing in disused Latrines. Parados on South Side of covered way near pulpit Sap made higher. Repaired Trenches in STAFFORD STREET.

Short Sap and parados in traverse at foot of LICHFIELD STREET. Trenches along front damaged by Trench Mortars repaired.

(sd) E.W.BAIRD.
BRIGADIER GENERAL,
Comdg 179th Inf. Bde.

July 17th 1916.

CONFIDENTIAL.

179th Infantry Brigade.

DAILY INTELLIGENCE SUMMARY - 10 a.m. 17/7/16 to 10 a.m. 18/7/16.

1. OPERATIONS: (a) M.G. indirect fire was brought to bear as under:-

M.O.D. Road A.17a. 2 - 5. Rounds 500.
Cross Roads A.4.d. 9 - 4. " 250.
M.O.C. Cross Roads LES TILLEULS at A.11a.9 - 9. Rounds 500.

Quiet on the whole during the day. Move activity from 11.30 p.m. to about 2.30 a.m. Trench Mortars sent over a few rounds chiefly for Ranging. At 11.30 p.m. and again at 2.10 a.m. fired at Point A.10.d. 6 - 4. Lewis Guns traversed Enemy parapets at intervals during the night.

(b) Desultory firing of Rifle Grenades, aerial torpedoes and Trench Mortars came over the objective principally being BENTATA Redoubt. Beyond this the Enemy fire was directed at no particular spot.

2. INTELLIGENCE. Enemy Working Parties heard during the night. Between 9 and 9.15 p.m. an explosion took place in Enemy Lines. The position as near as can be judged was about 600 yards on a bearing of ~~xxx~~ 85° taken from Junction of BIRAS SAP with DOUBLEMENT. One Enemy Working Party was engaged upon the construction of either a Sniper post or Machine Gun Emplacement which is being closely observed. A bearing is being taken of this. Enemy Sentry Post located at A.10.d.2.

3. GENERAL. A Patrol consisting of 2/Lieut. Gearing, Sgt. Carr and Pte. Babb, went out from BENTATA to see whether a Snipers Post ~~xxxxx~~ could be reconstructed on CLAUDOT ~~xxxxxx~~ (A.10.a. 7 - 4) but it was decided this could not be done. Captain Wills went out at 1.30 a.m. to examine our wire in front of BENTATA and it has been decided to strengthen in parts. Enemy fixed Rifle Post observed opposite Crater 810. A post is to be constructed to cover this. Enemy Snipers very quiet during whole period.

From BENTATA III Post one German was seen for a few seconds. A periscope subsequently appeared which was fired at.

4. WORK DONE. M. G. Emplacements improved and ration recess made at O.3, also rubbish pit. Repairing Trench damaged by shell fire at M.H. Removing Sandbags from Mine dump and filling in disused Latrines. STAFFORD ST. Parapets built up. Sap 60.b. revetted. Repairs made to bottom of LICHFIELD ST. damaged by T.M. Co. Dump cleared. Bomb Blocks improved in various places. Bridge shelters repaired in parts. Repairing parts of DOUAI.

HORSE.
July 18th 1916.

BRIGADIER GENERAL.
Comdg 179th Infantry Brigade.

179th Infantry Brigade.

WEEKLY INTELLIGENCE SUMMARY.

for week ending 18th July 1916.

....

GENERAL SUMMARY.

As a whole this Front has been quiet. Spasmodic bursts of Trench Mortaring taking place roughly twice in every 24 hours. BENTATA and the DOUAI Trench at Junction with ELBE being apparently particular objectives.

Retaliation when asked for has in every case been successful in silencing the Enemy in a short time.

Enemy Working Parties have been generally bold, returning to points from which they have been dispersed by either Lewis or Stokes Gun Fire about half an hour after dispersal.

Trucks have been heard moving in Enemy Lines and it is thought Trench Mortars are conveyed from point to point in this manner.

Enemy has been keenly alert for any movement in our line immediately sending over Bombs. Flares are practically continuous from Enemy Lines during the night. Generally the Enemy attitude appears to warrant belief in his reliance on mechanical appliances and that his line is thinly held by men.

The wind has not been favourable for Gas Attacks by Enemy.

The weather generally has not been favourable for observation.

Trenches generally are now fairly dry.

The majority of the Enemy seen appear to be youthful.

TRENCH MORTAR located at A.16b. ~~40xxx52x~~ 13 - 35.

MINENWERFER located at A.16b. 40 - 52.

OBSERVATION Post located at A.10d. 17 - 12.

SNIPERS BAGS. No kill is recorded.

HORSE.
July 19th 1916.

BRIGADIER GENERAL,
Comdg 179th Infantry Brigade.

CONFIDENTIAL: I.R.6.

179th Infantry Brigade.

DAILY INTELLIGENCE SUMMARY - 10 a.m. 18/7/16 to 10 a.m. 19/7/16.

1. OPERATIONS. No raid.

(a) M.G. indirect fire was brought to bear on following points:-

M.O.C. Gun on Cross Roads A.11c. 6 - 9. rounds 500.

" " " Common Trench A.10b. 8 - 8 to A.11a. 9 - 9. rounds 250.

M.O.D. " " A.11b. 5 - 1. rounds 500.

MEDIUM T.M's. 2" fired rounds 51.

L.T.M's. fired rounds 139.

Our Artillery fired several rounds at 2 p.m. and 5 p.m. at points unobservable. French Mortars active on Enemy front line opposite H.1, otherwise generally quiet.

(b) Enemy M.G. fairly active during the night, generally traversing our first line parapets throughout the sector. An aerial torpedo fell just at head of Sap 41a. doing no damage.

2. INTELLIGENCE. At 12.50 a.m. two very bright lights were observed N.E. of Sap 34a. Their intensity appeared to increase and when they ultimately died away, a trail of sparks remained clearly visible for over 3 minutes. Simultaneously with the disappearance of these spark trails, a green flare was sent up by Enemy due S. of Sap Head 34a.

At 1.45 a.m. two white balloons were seen travelling over Enemy Lines in a S.E. direction. At 7.30 a.m. 12 British Aeroplanes passed over Centre Sector flying due East - heavily shelled by Enemy.

An Enemy Working Party were observed opposite Sap 38a. Men were wearing grey caps and tunics. They were fired on and one man appeared to drop.

3. GENERAL. All night Sounds of Enemy Transport. Also the noise of a light engine. The direction appeared to be N.E. of head of Sap 45a.

Officers Patrol endeavoured to ascertain what an Enemy Working party were doing, but unsuccessfully.

4. WORK DONE. Revetting with Sand-bags in Sap 41.B. Various disused latrines filled in. Deepening Fire Trench near Junction BENTATA and Sap 38a. Firing Line Parapet and parados improved. CLAUDOT is being deepened in parts. Various M.G. Emplacements repaired.

(sd) H.W.BAIRD.

HORSE.
July 19th 1916.

BRIGADIER GENERAL,
Comdg 179th Infantry Brigade.

CONFIDENTIAL.

179th Infantry Brigade.

179th
No. M.115/7
Date 20/7/16
INFANTRY BRIGADE.

I.R.7½

DAILY INTELLIGENCE SUMMARY - 10 a.m. 19/7/16 to 10 a.m. 20/7/16.

****

1. OPERATIONS. No raid.

(a) M.G. indirect fire

From A 8 d 21.50 to A I I c 58 - 91		rounds	500.
A 15 a 05.68 to A 11 b 38.68		"	500
T.M.s fired			
No.1 gun at point	A 16c 9.7	"	7
" "	A 16a 9.2	"	5
" "	A 16c 8.8	"	9
No.2 gun "	A 10c 98.50	"	10
No.3 gun "	Registering	"	5
No.4 gun "	A 10c 90.83	"	7

(a) Artillery fairly active at times during afternoon, ranging and successful retaliation fire.

(b) Trench Mortars few only sent over during the morning. From 2 p.m. till 3.30 p.m. enemy shelled our Front M2 lines. A large number (estimate 40%) failed to explode and very little damage done to trenches. T.M's active along front of M2 about about 2.30 p.m. to 3.15 p.m.

Considerable damage was done by Trench Mortars to M.Gun position A 16a 08.08 gun and stores being buried but gun not damaged.

2. INTELLIGENCE. BENTATA REDOUBT appears to be a favourite objective of the enemy, as also DOUAI in a lesser degree.

A large number of rifle shots opposite M2 front were fired by enemy apparently at random at no definite target. An enemy working party at about A 10b 3 - 7 were dispersed by Lewis Gun at 1 a.m.

Nothing particular was observed with regard to flares or signals.

A number of our aeroplanes flew over about 7.30 a.m. in a fairly compact group. Numbers counted vary between 17 and 20. They were heavily shelled but none appear hit. Several returned betwe 8 and 8.45 a.m.

Further information is being sought regarding the 2 white balloons reported yesterday. Meantime it is suggested these were put up by enemy to test wind direction.

Enemy sniper located in crater opposite Sap 40 B. (A 10c9.9)

Artillery patrol out from 11.15 to 11.45 inspecting wire.

3. WORK DONE. Alternative emplacement improved at A 4c 39.28, and repairing of position A 16a 08.08.

Filling up old latrines - Filling sand bags at TERRITORIAL ISLAND generally repairing front line parapets, and various parts of ~~XXXXX~~ BENTATA - and deepening CLAUDOT in parts.

HORSE
July 20th 1916

(sd) [illegible] BAIRD
BRIGADIER GENERAL
Cmdg. 179th Infantry Brigade

CONFIDENTIAL.

179th Infantry Brigade.

DAILY INTELLIGENCE SUMMARY - 10 a.m. 20/7/1916 to 10 a.m. 21/7/1916.

1. OPERATIONS.

(a) No raid.

M.G. at A.15a.05.68 between 10.10 p.m. and 10.30 p.m. fired indirect at
CROSS ROADS A.5.c.10.20. Rounds 500.
and A.11a.90.85. " "
M.G. at A.8.d.21.50 between 10.15 and 10.45 p.m. at
A.17a.10.49 and
A.11a.0.72 to A.11a.90.85 Rounds 750.
L.T.M's fired " 212.
in conjunction with Artillery and M.T.M's between 4 and 4.40 p.m. on Enemy front lines from point opposite Sap 37a. to point opposite Sap.39b. Also retaliation fire and dispersing working parties out after dark, repairing ~~xxxkx~~ damage done by afternoon bombardment.

Bombardment of Enemy Lines opposite to Saps 37a. and 39b. from A.16a.92.58 to A.10d.01.33 between 4 p.m. and 4.40 p.m. and the Enemy front line appears to have been seriously damaged.

(b) Trench Mortars fairly active during the day in vicinity of A.16c.15.82 and A.10.c.31.10 otherwise firing was spasmodic and again directed on BRNTATO REDOUBT.

2. INTELLIGENCE.

(a) Enemy were heard working in the vicinity of Crater A.10c.84.82 at about 12 midnight. This party was observed and dispersed by Lewis Gun Fire.

Again at 3.20 a.m. a party in the same spot was dispersed.

Transport was distinctly heard during the night in THELUS. A red flare was sent up by the Enemy last night near A.16a.90.15 followed almost at once by a call like a wild duck which was repeated along the enemy line.

(b) Two Zeppelins were observed at 9.10 p.m. proceeding in a Northerly direction flying at a rapid rate and at a high altitude. Our Aeroplanes were active over lines during the day.

3. GENERAL. Sniperx claims 1 hit. Patrol of 1 Officer and 8 men surveyed wire in front of firing line M.1.

~~xxxyxx~~ Patrol of 1 Officer and 1 man surveyed wire in front of PULPIT.

4. WORK DONE. Improvements to Gower Street. Strengthening parapets generally along front line. Clearing debris caused by Enemy T.Ms. Work continued in ZIVY. New M.G. Emplacement making in GUILLERMOT and work progressed with New Sniping Post on W. of PULPIT. CLAUDOT Sap deepened and Fire Trench revetted in various places.

HORSE.
July 21st 1916.

BRIGADIER GENERAL,
Comdg 179th Inf. Brigade.

179th
No. 1178/8
21/7/16
I.B.S.
INFANTRY BRIGADE

CONFIDENTIAL:

179th Infantry Brigade.

DAILY INTELLIGENCE SUMMARY - 10 a.m. 21/7/16 to 10 a.m. 22/7/16.

1. OPERATIONS: (a) No raid.
M.G's. searched with indirect fire between 10.30p.m. and 11.45 p.m.
RAILWAY at A.17a.90.40.
TRENCH Junction at A.11b.35.05.
CROSS ROADS at A.11c.55.89.
ROAD at A.17a.90.10.
Salvos were fired on Enemy Support Trenches from a N line due EAST of SAP 37a. to a Line due EAST of SAP 39b. at 10.30 p.m. at 11.30 p.m. at 11.45 p.m. at 12.10 a.m. at 1.30 a.m. and at 1.45 a.m.
Light T.Ms. fired 162 rounds principally in retaliation and to disperse Working Parties.
H.T.Ms. were active at times during the day in retaliation.
(b) Aerial Torpedoes and Oil Cans were sent over in a desultory manner. T.Ms. were less active than yesterday. Heavy guns (8") were apparently searching for our Batteries in rear of Bde. H.Q.

2. INTELLIGENCE. Enemy appear to be particularly busy in the Crater at A.16a.85.10. Sounds of hammering in wood and iron distinctly heard.
At 11.50 a.m. a very bright light was seen for a period of 10 minutes, a very considerable distance away in a S.E. direction. Enemy Working parties are bold, returning again and again after dispersal.
Particular activity appeared to be behind SHEBAS BREASTS.

3. GENERAL. Patrols were out examining wire in various places, but were hampered by our own Artillery firing during last night. A patrol went out from Sap 35c. and confirmed report of activity of Enemy working party.

4. WORK DONE. ~~Exxxx~~ CLAUDOT and MIRPELLET deepened. ZIVY Redoubt improved. MILL ST. - MAITLAND ST. continued and general repair of front line parapets.
BAIRD STREET and DOUAI repaired in parts. MERCIER Trench repaired in parts.

BRIGADIER GENERAL,
Comdg. 179th Infantry Brigade.

HORSE.
July 22nd 1916.

I.R.10.

CONFIDENTIAL.

179th Infantry Brigade.

DAILY INTELLIGENCE SUMMARY - 10 a.m. 22/7/16 to 10 a.m. 23/7/16.

1. OPERATIONS.

(a). No raid.

M.Gs. searched CROSS ROADS at A.5.c.10.20 RAILWAY at ~~xx~~ A.17a.90.40 and points at A.11.c.55.89, at A.17.a.10.49 to A.17a.40.49.

L.T.Ms. and M.T.Ms. active at times along our front in retaliation. Artillery was called upon for retaliation fire on our right sector principally.

(b) At 12 noon Enemy very active with T.Ms. and from 1 till 2 p.m. our front was subjected to a really heavy bombardment Oilcans, Aerial Torpedoes, Rifle Grenades and Sling Bombs were all used. The points in our line which particularly suffered being at A.16a.45.30 (DOUAI) and at A.16.c.42.95.

From 10 p.m. till midnight Enemy were again very active with T.Ms. on a line of our ~~xxxxx~~ Front extending from A.10.c.56.10 to A.10.c.50.65.

Our retaliation fire was considered insufficient. Enemy M.Gs. swept our front line parapets at various times during the night.

A heavy Artillery Bombardment was heard away to the South lasting all night.

2. INTELLIGENCE.

A periscope was observed about 50 yards in front of our post at A.10.c.67.80, presumably indicating an Enemy Sap head. The Enemy appeared nervous or jumpy at "Stand to" this morning particularly from opposite to points A.16.c.75.75 to A.16.a.80.18.

There appeared to be a considerably less number of flares sent up last night by the Enemy except at "Stand to". Nine British Aeroplanes were observed at 8.5 p.m. flying in a Northerly direction.

3. GENERAL. A Sniper of the 2/14th L.R. went out at 3 a.m. to a spot 40 to 50 yards from Crater at A.16.a.85.9. Two Germans were seen and fired at by him and the German dropped suddenly. This Sniper declares that he saw a large T.M. Bomb hurled from the Crater. He watched carefully but saw nothing further and crawled back into Trench at 9 a.m. without having been apparxently seen.

An Officers Patrol went out to Crater at A.16.a.80.80 but nothing of import was noticed. ~~Patrol work last night was difficult as the absence of Very Lights rendered it nearly impossible to see anything.~~

4. WORK DONE. Trench cleared and parapet improved at A.4.c.39.28. Drainage and Ammunition (M.G.) improved in places. Repairing Trenches generally where damaged by Enemy bombardment. Cutting out and widening Walls in ground level of STAFFORD ST. filling Sandbags and Stacking on parapet of BROOK ST. Repairing and clearing Second ~~xxxxxxx~~ Stairway of ZIVY CAVE. Digging and clearing out under Trench Boards in DOUBLEMONT.

HORSE.
July 23rd 1916.

BRIGADIER GENERAL,
Comdg 179th Infantry Brigade.

CONFIDENTIAL: **I.R.11.**

179th Infantry Brigade.

DAILY INTELLIGENCE SUMMARY - 10 a.m. 23/7/16 to 10 a.m. 24/7/16.

1. **OPERATIONS.** (a) M.G. Fire was directed on points at A.13a.75.57 between 10 p.m. and 10.30 p.m. and at A.11a.90.85 between 10.15 and 10.30 p.m.

Our Light T.Ms. fired 110 rounds during the past 24 hours both in retaliation and at suspected T.M.points, at A.16a.85.15, and at A.16a.95.90.

Enemy Front Trench for about 20 yards was damaged in vicinity of point A.4d.35.35.

No.4 M.T.M. Gun is temporarily Out-of-action.

(b) Enemy T.Ms. were active between 12.30 and 1 p.m. firing round about point A.16a.09.09. and A.16c.16.82. From 4.10 to 4.35 p.m. T.Ms. were again active in vicinity of A.4c.40.28. Artillery, Oilcans, Sling Bombs and Rifle Grenades were all used at various points along our front.

Retaliation was asked for from the firing line along our front and in all cases when given it was quite inadequate. The usual Enemy M.G.fire swept our parapets during the night.

2. **INTELLIGENCE.** (a) A German was observed wearing a red and gold laced hat at A.16a.85.10. At 3.30 a.m. a noise like the working of a drill driven by an Engine was heard but it was impossible to locate.. It is suggested that the heavy Bombardment by the Enemy yesterday afternoon was owing to their thinking a relief was taking place.

A German was observed opposite Sap.42b. at 10.15 a.m. wearing a Khaki Tunic and Cap, age about 40. He was shot at and fell sideways instantly. The body was removed in about 4 minutes and shortly afterwards a mop-head was put up in same spot under a cap and worked slowly from side to side to draw, it is suggested, our fire, but unsuccessfully. Our aircraft were fairly active during the day.

(b) An Enemy Aeroplane was driven off about 7.30 p.m. by 3 British Machines. He disappeared over THELUS. Flares were much less in evidence last night than usual.

3. **GENERAL.** (a) One British Officer and three Sowars of 29th Lancers reconnoitred from dark till 1 a.m. in vicinity of PULPIT. Reported no signs of Enemy working.

1 N.C.O. and eight men reconnoitred from SAP 42b. and reported no sign of Enemy holding Crater opposite.

(b) Enemy Patrol of four men dispersed by an Officer and Sergeant at a point opposite SAP 43a. by Bombing. No casualty to Enemy observed.

4. **WORKS DONE.** Damage to ZIVY Redoubt repaired and work on second entrance to ZIVY CAVE continued. Repairing parapets and fire steps badly damaged in various places along whole front. Wire gooseberries placed in position in several Saps. Several Latrines repaired and some fresh rubbish pits made.

NORSE.
July 24th 1916.

BRIGADIER GENERAL,
Comdg 179th Infantry Brigade.

CONFIDENTIAL. I.R.12.

179th Infantry Brigade.

DAILY INTELLIGENCE SUMMARY - 10 a.m. 24/7/16 to 10 a.m. 25/7/16.

1. OPERATIONS. (a) Indirect fire by our Machine Guns was conducted between 10 and 11 p.m. on
CROSS ROADS A.11.a.95.98.
" " A.11.b.60.75.
" " A.11.c.56.89.

Our L.T.M's fired 128 rounds in retaliation at various points particularly in the vicinity of A.10.c.90.60 and A.10.b.40.22 The night was quiet on the whole.

Our M.T.M's fired 20 rounds retaliation and also did some registering.

(b) Enemy were unusually quiet yesterday until about 5 p.m. when a number of Aerial Torpedoes came over at various points of our Front. The artillery was also used by Enemy in retaliation fire.

The usual machine Gun fire was opened at various times during the night on our front line parapet.

2. INTELLIGENCE.(a) An object looking like a large periscope has been observed at A.10.c.90.78 and it is believed to work in conjunction with a Trench Mortar. This object is having Sniper's careful attention.

Single red lights were sent up at 10 p.m. and again at 1 a.m. but no action followed. Less flares were used by the Enemy than usual. Our wire to the right of GOWER ST. in A.4.d. was damaged, but has been temporarily repaired.

(b) Between 4.15 and 5 p.m. intermittent shelling by Enemy on our Support Line took place about Junction of MERCIER and ASHTON St. and a few desultory shells came over at about ½ hour intervals until midnight. Otherwise Enemy activity was much less than the previous day.

3. GENERAL. Patrol of one Officer and 3 men (29th Lancers) left at 11 p.m. from Junction of LICHFIELD and GOWER ST. to examine Enemy wire and remained in Observation until 12.45 a.m. One German was seen working at their line.

Another Patrol of same Regiment started from end of FROGER Trench at 10.45 p.m. to locate a Sniper's Post. Sniper fired once and the shot sounded close. Further patrolling in the same direction on the knowledge of ground now acquired may prove successful.

An Officer Patrol went out from SAP 39a. but reported having seen nothing.

Listening Patrol went out and reported all quiet.

4. WORK DONE. Excavating for rubbish pits at A.16.c.16.82 at A.16.a. 11.85, and at A.10.c.34.12. M.G. Emplacements repaired and Trench Boards relaid in various parts. Revetting and deepening of BAIRD ST., DOUAI. Wiring done at A.10.c.70.70 and thereabouts and wire in front of Firing Line strengthened in parts.

(sd) E.W.BAIRD.

HORSE. BRIGADIER GENERAL
July 25th 1916. Comdg. 179th Infantry Brigade.

W.I.S. 2.

179th Infantry Brigade.

WEEKLY INTELLIGENCE SUMMARY.

For week ending 25th July 1916.

GENERAL SUMMARY:

No raiding has taken place this week.

There has been a marked increase in activity on this Front since the submission of last week's report. Desultory firing by the Enemy of Rifle Grenades, Aerial Torpedoes and Trench Mortars etc. at the beginning of the week quickened into that marked activity with Oil-cans, Trench Mortars, Aerial Torpedoes, Rifle Grenades and Sling Bombs, which reached the culminating point on the night of 22/23rd instant. BENTATA, PARIS REDOUBT, and DOUAI TRENCH suffered considerably. The retaliation given did not prove effectual on two occasions.

Enemy Working Parties have been persistent; a light engine has been heard; there has been marked activity in Crater at A.16 a.86.10 where work in wood and iron is in progress. All indications point to a still greater reliance by the Enemy on mechanical means to hold the line as a substitute for men.

The Trenches are now dry.

Nothing particular with regard to Light Signals has been noted.

Patrols and Working Parties have been out nightly examining Enemy wire and repairing our own; also endeavouring to locate particular centres of Enemy activity.

The general attitude of the Enemy appears altered since the night of the 23/24 and it is thought there is a different Regiment opposite.

It is suggested that the period of marked Enemy activity noted above may have covered a relief movement.

MINENWERFER has been located at A.16a.88.07, and
TRENCH MORTAR EMPLACEMENT has been discovered at A.10.d.00.30.
SNIPERS BAGS: 3 hits claimed.

HORSE.
July 26th 1916.

BRIGADIER GENERAL,
Comdg 179th Infantry Brigade.

CONFIDENTIAL.

179th Infantry Brigade.

DAILY INTELLIGENCE SUMMARY - 10 a.m. 25/7/16 to 10 a.m. 26/7/16.

1. **OPERATIONS.** (a) Quiet reigned along our Front yesterday only broken by occasional Enemy Trench Mortaring.

Indirect M.G. Fire was brought to bear on the following positions:-
Enemy Dump at A.12.d.84.89 and on
Points A.17.b.30.45. and A.17.d.70.40.
between 10 and 11 p.m.

T.Ms. from some Point in M.1 Sector fired at a point believed to be an emplacement at A.16.a.76.01. Our T.Ms. fired at the same place but the Emplacement did not appear to be hit. Our Stokes Guns endeavoured to knock out a loop-holed Emplacement at Point A.10.d.00.30 but unsuccessfully. This spot is having further close attention.

Our Stokes Guns fired 20 rounds between 4 and 5 ~~fxxm~~ p.m. on SHEBAS BREASTS doing considerable damage thereto.

(b) Enemy Artillery ranging in forenoon and somewhat active about 5 p.m. on various centres to the rear of our front lines. Enemy T.Ms. fired several rounds in ZIVY REDOUBT.

2. **INTELLIGENCE.** The large periscope reported yesterday was fired on by two of our Rifle Grenades, which however did not appear to hit. The periscope was ~~however~~ at once removed. It has been noticed that Rifle Grenades are fired by the Enemy on a system working from left to right along our Front Line; two or three shots being fired in quick succession at the same spot. Before each shot a noise was heard like the snap of a spring lid on a box.

At 2 a.m. two red flares were sent up by Enemy opposite point A.16.a.70.00 followed five minutes later by two green, two red, and then two green. Immediately after followed a Bombardment well to our left. Upon two more green flares going up the bombardment was noticed to cease.

About 2 AM An explosion was thought to have occurred at some distance away on the left. An aeroplane was seen flying very low over Enemy Lines travelling East.

Three of the Enemy were observed yesterday afternoon wearing Field Grey Uniform and and Cap flat with red edging. Owing to the distance away it is impossible to say definitely but through the glasses available the number on the Cap fronts looked like 62.

3. **GENERAL.** Patrol of two men went out from Sap 37.b. at 10 p.m. on the night of the 24th to Enemy Line opposite, and returned at 9 a.m. 25th instant. They reported having passed through two Enemy Listening Posts and located 4 Enemy T.Ms. in advance of the Enemy Front Line.

The area in which these T.Ms. are fixed is between A.16.a.90.65 and A.16.a.90.80. These men report that the Enemy front is very strongly wired (thick wire) but has a big gap in it at a point due EAST of head of SAP B.37.b. [37b] No sound of life in Enemy front line except at listening posts and at the T.M.Emplacements mentioned.

A Patrol of 1 N.C.O. and 4 men went out from Sap 43A at 10.45 p.m. A listening Patrol went out from Sap 43.b. at 11.30 p.m. returning at 12.30 a.m. Both had nothing to report.

One of the post at Sap 39.b. observing that particular quietness reigned, went out at 3 p.m. to the Eastern Lip of CLAUDOT CRATER and returned at 3.7 p.m. reporting that there was no sign of Enemy Occupation.

A Patrol of the 29th Lancers, one Officer and two men went out at 11.15 p.m. SHORTSAP N. of PULPIT to reconnoitre and if possible secure a prisoner. They observed a German Patrol consisting of at least eight men who were crawling towards our Line. Our Patrol taking these to be an Enemy Bombing Party returned to Sap-head, warned the Sentry and subsequently had a Lewis Gun turned on the ground upon which the Enemy party were likely to be. Before it was possible to ascertain if there were any Enemy casualties, a vigorous Enemy T.M. fire on our front line in the vicinity was ~~xxxxxxxx~~ opened.

4. <u>WORK DONE</u>. (a) Deepening BAIRD ST. and building Traverse. Sandbag revetting of RAWSON and ARGYLE ST. CLAUDOT SAP ~~xx~~ deepened and tunnel repaired. New Latrine in VISSEC SAP commenced. Firing Line revetted in various places. Clearing ZIVY Avenue and EDINBURGH ST. of debris caused by Enemy shelling. Dividing long Fire Step into bays with Sand-bags.

Constructing barricade in GOWER ST. SAP and improving Sentry Shelters.

(b) Observed to be constructing Loop-holes ~~xxxxxxx~~ opposite CLAUDOT SAP.

HORSE.
July 26th 1916.

BRIGADIER GENERAL,
Comdg 179th Infantry Brigade.

CONFIDENTIAL.

179th Infantry Brigade.

DAILY INTELLIGENCE SUMMARY - 10 a.m. 26/7/16 to 10 a.m. 27/7/16.

1. OPERATIONS. (a) The past 24 hours has been a period of general inactivity, our artillery firing only a very few rounds, except a small bombardment about 9 to 9.30 p.m. on to some spot on our left.
Two of our Machine Guns brought indirect fire to bear on
CROSS ROADS at A 11 a 95.98 and
CROSS ROADS at A 11 b 60.75
TRENCHES ...at A 17 d 15.60
TRENCHES ...at A 11 b 38.08
Our Trench Mortars fired at various enemy earthworks particularly at SHEBAS BREASTS and in retaliation of an occasional shot.

(b) Enemy artillery particularly quiet indulging only in a few desultory shots during the day, and occasional Trench Mortars up to midnight after which all was quiet.
Enemy Machine Guns did the usual traversing along our parapets. The enemy scored a hit on one of our Trench Mortars positions burying the gun, but gun undamaged, the cleaning rod and clinometer only being smashed.

2. INTELLIGENCE. An explosion took place about 9 p.m. last night on our left, followed by the artillery fire already mentioned.
About 9.30 p.m. two red lights went up when artillery fire slackened, then two green lights were seen.
Working was heard in enemy line opposite A 16 a 70.30.
Very few flares went up last night, the mist which was fairly thick rendering Very lights almost useless after 11 p.m.

(b) Enemy transport was distinctly heard N. of THELUS between 11 p.m. and midnight.
On e of the enemy was observed wearing grey, no facings or equipment, small round soft cap with a light grey band.
A working party was observed in enemy reserve line all wearing flat caps and blue overalls.

3. GENERAL. A patrol of 1 N.C.O. and 4 men went out to reconnoitre from Sap 43 b at 10.45 p.m. and reported presence of strong enemy patrols on left and right flanks.
1 N.C.O. and 3 men went out from PHILLIP STREET to reconnoitre crater opposite and reported no sign of enemy occupation.
Two men crawled out early ~~this~~ Yesterday morning to a point between the two craters at the end of Saps 35 B and 35 D to try and get a shot at an enemy sniper who had been active - but attempt was unsuccessful.
They report that the enemy have fortified the crater opposite and that there are several snipers posts erected.
A further reconnaisance of this particular spot will be made.

4. WORK DONE. Reconnaisance of disused trenches with a view to selecting good positions from which to snipe or observe.
Three positions have been selected.
Deepening BAIRD and HERD STREETS. Revetting parts of Firing Line and deepening CLAUDOT Sap.
Improving drainage in DOUBLEMONT Continuance of sentry shelters in GOMER ST.

HORSE
July 27th 1916.

BRIGADIER GENERAL
Comdg. 179th Infantry Brig

CONFIDENTIAL.

179th Infantry Brigade.

DAILY INTELLIGENCE SUMMARY - 10 a.m. 27/7/16 to 10 a.m. 28/7/16.

1. OPERATIONS.
(a) Past 24 hours quiet. Moderate activity T.Ms. during afternoon. From 12 to 1 p.m. Enemy Support Lines were shelled at intervals.

Indirect Machine Gun fire was brought to bear on Dump at THELUS A.12.d.84 - 89 on Light Railway at A.17.b.30.45 and on PATHWAY A.17.d.70.40.

Our M.T.M's fired 128 rounds at the following points:-
A.16.d.90.15. Damaging Trench at this spot.
A.10.d.10.40. Retaliation on Enemy Mortar.
A.10.b.30.80. to A.10.B.40.60. damaging Trenches.
A.4.d.40.40. on Enemy working party at night.

(b) Enemy Artillery Fire was practically NIL. From 8 to 8.30 p.m. a few Oilcans came over to a spot in the vicinity of A.16.c.50.55.

At 4 a.m. Enemy fired several T.Ms. on to BENTATA and CLAUDOT. Damage to our Trenches was slight. From 9.30 to 10.30 p.m. Enemy T.Ms. directed a desultory fire upon our front line between SAPS 43a and 43b. Only slight damage accrued.

2. INTELLIGENCE.
The night was remarkable on account of the extraordinary small number of Lights sent up by the Enemy. A fairly dense mist may partly account for this. During the early morning a Snipers plate was brought up by the Enemy and moved from place to place before a position was finally settled upon.

When sufficiently light the plate was fired at, appeared to split and fall back.

3. GENERAL. (a) A Patrol consisting of 1 N.C.O. and 3 men went out at 10.15 p.m. to examine the Crater at A.16.c.50.60 and returned at 11.15 p.m. reporting no sign of Enemy Working.

At 11 p.m. a Patrol of 1 Officer and 12 men went out to inspect wire S. of Sap 41.a. but returned reporting Night was too dark and misty for inspection.

At midnight a listening Patrol of one Officer and 4 men went out to a Point about 25 yards N. of Enemy Sap at A.4.d.35.35 and reported that all was quiet.

(b) A hostile Patrol, small numbers not discernible, came near our Post at SAP Head 34a. The night was extremely dark and misty. Our Sentry fired and threw 3 Bombs dispersing the party.

4. WORK DONE. (a) Improving parapets of Firing Line in various places. Cooking place dug at A.15.b. 11.50. Strengthening of barricades and Sentrry Shelter in GOWER ST. Digging Short C.T. from ZIVY AVENUE to West Spring Gun position. Continuing of BAIRD ST. deepening and deepening of further parts of CLAUDOT.

(b) Fresh earth thrown up in Enemy Trench at point A.4.d.35.15, evidently repairing damage done by Artillery fire.

HORSE.
July 28th 1916.

BRIGADIER GENERAL,
Comdg 179th InfantryBrigade.

I.R.15.

CONFIDENTIAL.

179th Infantry Brigade.

DAILY INTELLIGENCE SUMMARY - 10 a.m. 28/7/16 to 10 a.m. 29/7/16.

1. OPERATIONS.

(a) Yesterday was rather more active along our Front. Heavy Artillery fire from about 10.15 to 10.45 p.m. was directed to a spot on our left, where an Enemy Mine was blown shortly after 10 p.m.

Yesterday morning during the mist certain of our Machine Guns fired indirect on CROSS ROADS at A.11.c.58.89 and at A.11.b.60.75; also on Road from A.10.b.81.83 to A.11.a.90.90 and at points A.5.c.11.21 and A.11.a.95.98.

At 6.15 p.m. our Garrisons were withdrawn at the request of the Artillery from SAPS MERPILLAT and VISSEC, and certain Guns were registered.

Our Stokes Guns were fairly active between 7.30 and 9 p.m. firing on point at A.10.c.90.92 as noise of Enemy Working Party was heard thereabout.

(b) In the afternoon the Enemy Artillery paid more than usual attention to our Support Line with Shrapnel but the majority of Shells burst very high. The Enemy T.Ms. were also more vigorous especially between 9 and 10.30 p.m. The fire was accurate rather badly damaging Sap 39a at A.10.c.55.12 and BENTATA also came in for its recent customary share. M.G. firex was observed to sweep our Front Line parapets almost continuously for some minutes just after the Mine explosion took place.

2. INTELLIGENCE.

(a) A Squadron of our Aeroplanes flying Eastwards about 8 p.m. was heavily shelled by the Enemy; one was struck and feal slowly to the ground but where it landed (on our right) cannot be stated.

(b) A search light, the position of which was not located was used by Enemy from time to time during the Night, evidently searching for hostile Aircraft.

At 10.10 p.m. 3 Red Flares were sent up on our left, followed by Artillery Fire. At 11.5 p.m. two Green Lights went up when Artillery Fire ceased.

3. GENERAL. (a) Two prisoners, alive, were taken just in front of SAP 34.b. at 4.30 a.m. and despatched to Brigade Headquarters about 6 a.m.

A Patrol (Indian) went out from SAP 39.a. at 11 p.m. and returned at 12.30 a.m. having nothing to report.

A Patrol for inspecting wire went out from our left Sector and reported that the wire in front of Firing Line was in good state, only a few loose strands requiring seeing to.

(b) About a a.m. a party of from 4 to 6 of the Enemy approached our line at A.16.a.85.80. They were driven off without doing any damage and as far as could be observed suffered no casualties. This mist which was dense this early morning made Observation almost impossible.

4. WORK DONE. (a) Altering and strengthening posts in SAP 34A, 35A, and 35B. Repairing ARGYLE ST. and VICTORIA AVENUE. SAP 35A is particularly badly damaged but wire obstacles were temporarily erected during the day. Clearing LOSANGE TRENCH where it collapsed. Strengthening SAP 41A. Improving parapets in STOKE St. Filling in old Dug-Outs in GOWER ST.

(b) Fresh Enemy wire seen at A.4.d.30.55 and also new Sand bags immediately behind. Enemy fresh Sand bags noticed at A.10.c.99.20.

I.R.16.

CONFIDENTIAL.

179th Infantry Brigade.

DAILY INTELLIGENCE SUMMARY - 10 a.m. 29/7/16 to 10 a.m. 30/7/16.

1. OPERATIONS. (a) The last 24 hours have been more active than for some days past. At 5 p.m. our Artillery and Trench Mortars bombarded the Enemy Support and Front Line Trenches, giving particular attention to points where hostile T.Ms. had been located. The bombardment lasted for 20 minutes, the first minute being intensive.

The shooting was apparently accurate and damaging. The targets aimed at were Trench A.16.c.75.82 to A.16.c.95.80, Trench A.16.c.95.30 to A.16.d.10.80, Trenches A.16.c.95.80 to A.16.a.95.10 and A.16.d.10.80 to A.16.b.10.10 and A.16.c.90.90 to A.16.d.05.70. Particular points to which the 4.5" Hows. paid attention are A.16.c.95.80 and A.16.d.05.70 and A.16.d.10.80.

During the bombardment the hostile front line Trenches behind ARGYLE CRATER were subjected to a hot T.M.Fire and much wood-work was observed to go up. During the night our Stokes Guns kept firing at intervals of about 30 minutes commencing at 10 p.m. on various points noted during the afternoon bombardment. A fire was observed to occur after one of our shots @ A.4.d.40.40 between 10 p.m & 2.30 am 202 rds were fired.

(b) The Enemy retaliation was feeble consisting of T.Ms. and particularly Aerial Torpedoes. Damage to our Trenches was slight. From 9 to 11 p.m. Enemy T.Ms. were active firing principally on BENTATA and CLAUDOT SAPS.

2. INTELLIGENCE. (a) An Enemy Gun - position in the direction of VIMY- is very annoying being able to enfilade Trenches on M.2. An object resembling an Accumulator Battery appeared in Enemy Sap-head directly opposite SAP 38a. but must have been hit during the bombardment as it is now a broken mass of planks and sacking. At 2.15 a.m. cries of "KAMARADE of MINE" coming from point near Sap-head 36A, but the shouts were so loud (plainly heard for 200 yards) that it was considered a possible Hun ruse to draw some of our men to the open, and no notice was consequently taken.

(b) An Aeroplane (Enemy) of an uncommon type passed over our lines about 2.30 p.m. flying in the direction of MAROEUIL. It was constructed of a very light coloured fabric, having a large blue cross painted on the under-wings. Two Enemy Observation balloons were up, far back.

A pocket book taken from a dead German found in mending RAWSON ST. is forwarded for examination.

At 8.45 p.m. Enemy sent up three white flares in a bunch. No action followed.

3. GENERAL. Two Patrols went out each of two men, one from FROGER SAP and the other from SHORT SAP at about 11 p.m. and returned about 2 a.m. The object of both patrols was to obtain a prisoner. They reported no movement on the part of the Enemy near them. Both Patrols laid down close up to Enemy Front-Line Trench. They heard the noise of tools in Enemy Trenches and the rumble of iron wheels on rails. The way the Enemy are now working their flares is; one man patrols a given length of Trench letting off a light at different points on his beat. Both Patrols further reported that a considerable amount of Signalling by mouth whistling appeared to go on.

Snipers' Reports in original attached.

4. WORK DONE. Strengthening GRANDE BRETELLE, rebuilding parapet in DOUBLEMENT. Repairs to RAWSON ST. Saps 34A, 35A & 36B, also to ARGYLE ST. Repairing FROGER Sap and parts of BENTATA. New wiring done between CLAUDOT and FROGER Sap heads.

I.R.17.

CONFIDENTIAL.

179th Infantry Brigade.

DAILY INTELLIGENCE SUMMARY - 10 a.m. 30/7/16 to 10 a.m. 31/7/16.

1. **OPERATIONS.** (a) With the exception of a bombardment about 1 a.m. by our artillery on some point to our left, the period under review has been quiet on the whole. Our T.Ms. fired retaliation between A.16.c.90.10 and A.16.c.10.90 and good results were observed from two shots in particular. No.4 Gun is temporarily out of action owing to a broken bed. Our Light T.Ms. did some retaliatory fire on A.16.b.40.40. with success and bombed Snipers post at A.16.a.55.15 and ~~xxx~~ caused an Enemy T.M. to cease operations by firing at A.10.d. 15.75. Our Machine Guns indulged in some indirect fire on CROSS ROADS LES TILLEULS A.11a.90.90. and at A.17.a.09.50 and at A.18.a.75.67, the latter being CROSS ROADS at THELUS.

(b) Enemy put about 12 rounds T.Ms. into our Right Sector Support Line at midday, and at intervals during the afternoon, traversed our front line (Right Sector) with whizz-bangs. S.1 had several Aerial Torpedoes over it between 9 and 10 p.m.

2. **INTELLIGENCE.** (a) In a wood near BRAY a note was picked up of which the following is a copy:-

To the R.F.C.

The wreath dropped by the British Flying Corps for Lieutenant Immelmann will be laid down on his Grave Der am 19/7/16 Vormittag Notgelandete Obdt. H. Clements, R.Fl.C. ist unverwundet in gefangenschaft geraten.

German Flying Corps.

Tapping was heard underneath Post at A.16.c.45.75. It was reported to a Mining Officer who confirmed. A German Working Party was observed due East of A.16.a.50.30, wearing Caps similar to those worn by the prisoners captured two days ago. The large periscope or Camera Obscura, opposite VIMEO (A.10.c.90.80) is still obvious and it is suggested this point be given ~~a dose of fire~~.* by heavy Battery Fire It has been noticed recently that when we put up a Very Light the ~~xxxxx~~ Enemy frequently reply to the point from which they think the Light was sent up with a Rifle Grenade.

An Enemy Aeroplane flew over our Front Lines about 4.30 p.m. and again at 6.55 p.m. but was not fired upon by our Anti-Aircraft Guns.

3. **GENERAL.** A Patrol of 1 N.C.O. and 4 men went out from SAP 34A at 1 a.m. returning at 2 a.m. They inspected Snipers Plates at about A.16.a.57.85 and found them very firmly embeded. In size and shape they are similar to our own, the principal difference noted being that they have an oblong slit at the bottom right hand corner. This patrol then crawled round edge of Crater at end of Sap 34A and found that it was connected with a disused Trench running towards German Lines by a shallow sap, protected with Knife Rests. Inside the CRATER a ledge runs round the lip about 5' below the top rim.

It must be an easy matter for the Enemy to get into this CRATER under cover. ~~A sketch is attached hereto.~~ At 10 p.m. a Patrol consisting of 1 N.C.O. and 4 men went out from Sap. 37B. to inspect Enemy wire immediately in front. They reported that it was in good condition and very thick.

An Officers Patrol went out about 2 a.m. to ARGYLL GROUP of Craters to endeavour to prove if an Enemy Patrol upon which fire had been directed the previous night, had caused a casualty as it was confidently thought one Enemy was hit. A body was found, but his tunic had no identification marks and he had apparently been out without Equipment and unarmed. The enclosed papers were found on him and the button was cut off his tunic.

4. WORK DONE. (a) Rubbish Pit dug at A.10.c.84.12. Trench drained near A.8.d.21.50. Machine Gun Emplacement improved near A.4.c.09.09.

Wiring in front of SAP 34.A. and 60.a. repaired. Damaged Trenches STAFFORD ST. and DOUBLEMENT repaired. Continuance of Sentry Shelters in GRAND BRETELLE.

(b) New Earth Works and Wire opposite BENTATA SAP.

Bde. H.Q.
July 31st 1916.

BRIGADIER GENERAL,
Comdg 179th Infantry Brigade.

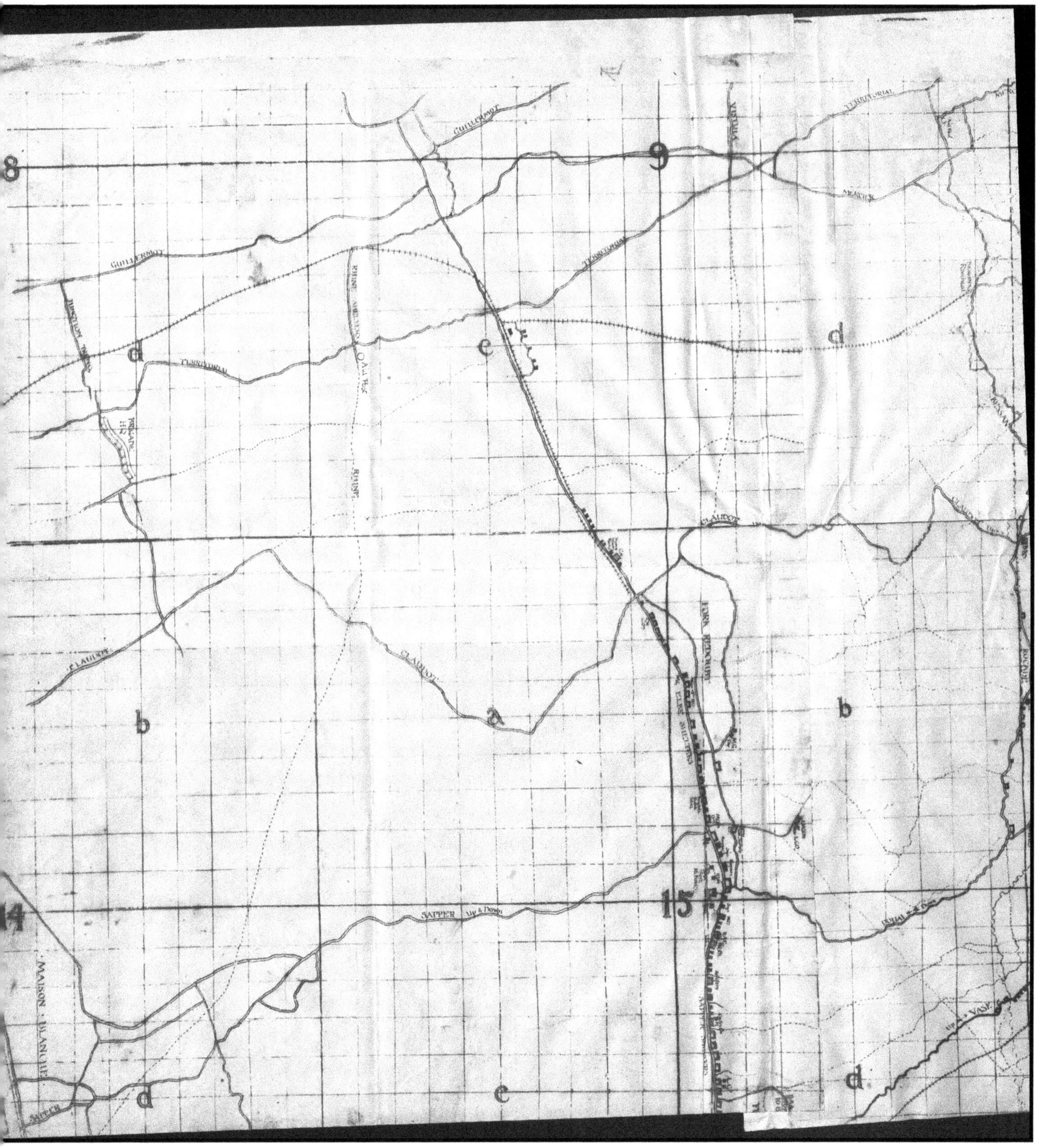

8
9
14
15
GUILLEMONT
TERRITORIAL
MERCIER
CLAUDOT
SAPPER Up & Down
MAISON BLANCHE
a
b
c
d

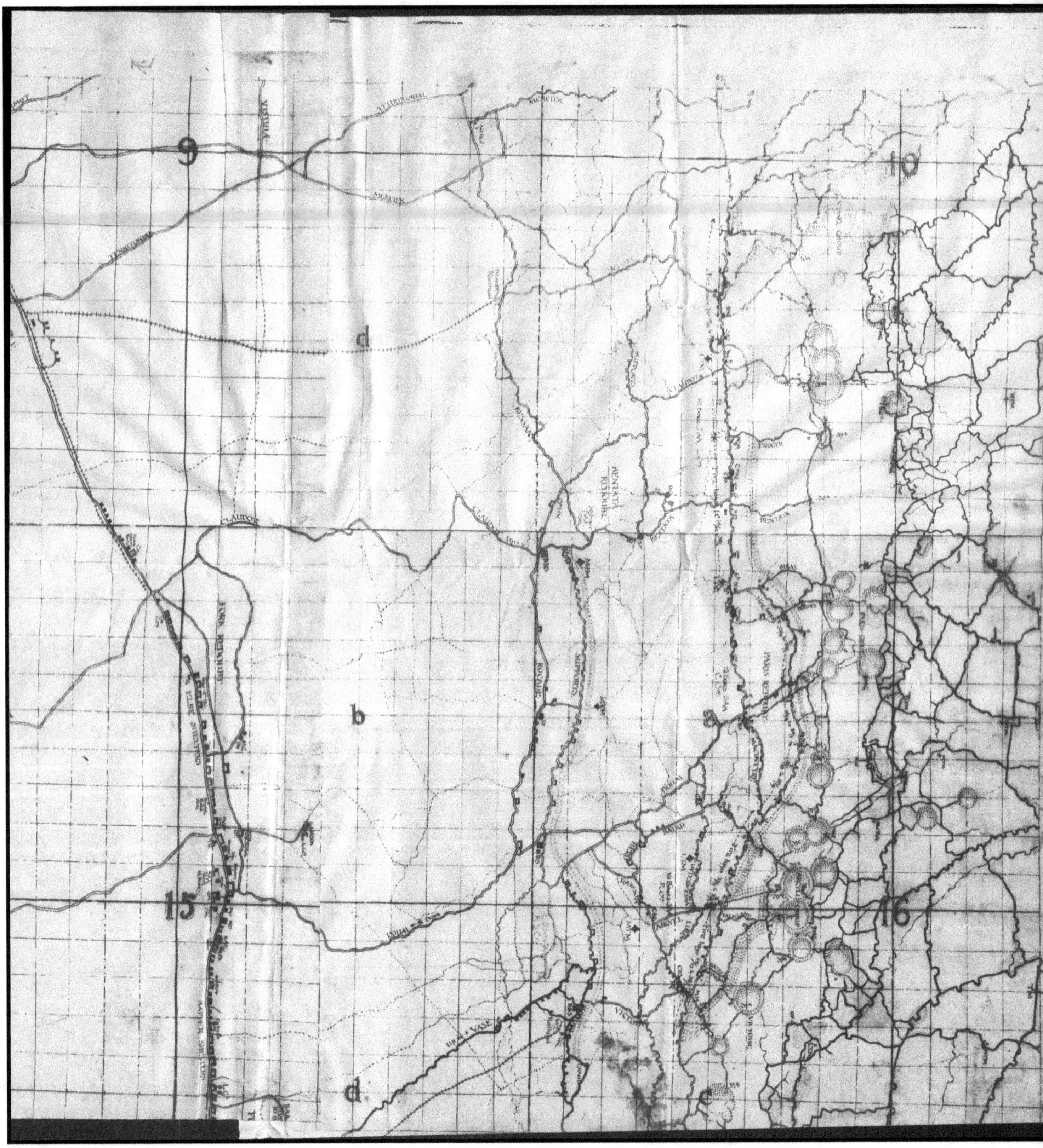

9
10
d
b
15
16
d

179th Bde
July 1916

179 1829

July 16.

Confidential

VOL. III

WAR DIARY Vol 3

OF

179TH INFANTRY BRIGADE

FROM 1ST AUGUST, 1916 TO 31ST AUGUST, 1916

Instructions regarding War Diaries and Intelligence Summaries are contained in F. S. Regs., Part II. and the Staff Manual respectively. Title Pages will be prepared in manuscript.

179th Inf. Bde

WAR DIARY
or
INTELLIGENCE SUMMARY
(Erase heading not required.)

August 1916

Vol III

Army Form C. 2118

Place	Date	Hour	Summary of Events and Information	Remarks and references to Appendices
TRENCHES near NEUVILLE ST VAAST	1st		Enemy inactive except for Trench Mortars which appear to have moved from opposite right subsector to the left of the left-subsector	
	2nd		Very quiet - nothing to record	
	3rd		Our artillery practised wire cutting on enemy's support line. Their firing line is too close to our own to allow guns to cut wire in front of it without withdrawing troops. Our Trench mortars were active and the enemy's retaliation weak	
	4th		The battalions in support and reserve relieved the battalions in the firing line in the early hours of the morning. The enemy shelled the Cross roads and dumps at NEUVILLE ST VAAST from 1.0pm to 5.0pm little damage however was done.	
	5th		A normal day with a certain amount of artillery activity. Our Heavy Corps Artillery bombarded a strongly fortified crater known as SHEBAS POINT. Only one direct hit was observed and this only hit a corner of the concrete cupola which evidently exists in the crater.	

1875 Wt. W593/826 1,000,000 4/15 J.B.C. & A. A.D.S.S./Forms/C. 2118.

Instructions regarding War Diaries and Intelligence Summaries are contained in F. S. Regs., Part II. and the Staff Manual respectively. Title Pages will be prepared in manuscript.

WAR DIARY
or
INTELLIGENCE SUMMARY
(Erase heading not required.)

Army Form C. 2118

Place	Date	Hour	Summary of Events and Information	Remarks and references to Appendices
TRENCHES near NEUVILLE St VAAST	6th		A quiet day. At 10.30 pm a raid was made on the enemy trenches. A detailed account of this is shewn in Appendix VI	
	7th		A quiet day. After dark search parties were sent out to look for those missing from the raid on the previous night. The officer Lieut [illegible] leader of the raid and three men, all wounded, were found. See Appendix VI.	Appendix VII
	8.		Nothing to record.	
	9.		Nothing to record	
	10.		Preparations were made for the explosion of a mine near a sap head called the Pulpit. This was necessary as our listeners in system of mines in that locality had discovered a German gallery being worked towards our lines and it was thought that he might anyday charge and blow. The time was fixed for 12.30 am. as it was hoped that at this hour there would be a chance of catching a German shift at work. Orders for the blowing of the mine and consolidating of the crater are shewn in Appendix VII	
	11.		The mine was exploded at 12.30 am. and the crater occupied without any opposition except sniping. The crater was much larger than was expected	Appendix VII

1875 Wt. W593/826 1,000,000 4/15 J.B.C. & A. A.D.S.S./Forms/C. 2118.

Instructions regarding War Diaries and Intelligence Summaries are contained in F. S. Regs., Part II. and the Staff Manual respectively. Title Pages will be prepared in manuscript.

WAR DIARY
or
INTELLIGENCE SUMMARY
(Erase heading not required.)

Army Form C. 2118

Place	Date	Hour	Summary of Events and Information	Remarks and references to Appendices
TRENCHES NEUVILLE ST VAAST	11 Con.		and the posts which were made during the night were found to be untenable by daylight. The detailed account of the raid is given in the Officer Commanding 2/13th Battn London Regts report attached to Appendix VII	Appendix VII
	12th		A day of marked activity with Trench Mortars and Guns on both sides. The consolidation of the crater was continued at night but as reliefs were carried out in the early hours of the morning work was rather interrupted	
	13th		A quiet day. Good work done on the new crater during the night a second sap out to it was cleared by opening out an old French trench which had been filled with wire.	
	14th		Our trench mortars were active especially the Stokes guns. The work on the new crater was continued during the night	
	15th		Our artillery in conjunction with trench mortars bombarded the enemy lines in places where trench mortars were reported to be in position near the THELUS Road	
	16		A quiet day. Nothing to record	
	17th		A short bombardment of enemy line was carried out from 6.0 pm to 6.10 pm	

Instructions regarding War Diaries and Intelligence Summaries are contained in F. S. Regs., Part II. and the Staff Manual respectively. Title Pages will be prepared in manuscript.

WAR DIARY
or
INTELLIGENCE SUMMARY
(Erase heading not required.)

Army Form C. 2118

Place	Date	Hour	Summary of Events and Information	Remarks and references to Appendices
TRENCHES NEUVILLE ST VAAST	17th (cont)		Target trenches behind EDINBOROUGH Crater	
	18th		A patrol of 2 men of 2/14th The London Regiment reconnoitred the enemy line during daylight and located an enemy heavy T.M. in a Crater of the POPE'S group. This crater is evidently held by a small post	
	19th		A quiet day nothing to record	
	20th		The 2/15th and 2/16th were relieved in the line by 2/14th and 2/13th. The relief took place in the early hours of the morning and was completed by 8.30 am without casualties	
	21st		Our trench mortars were active otherwise a quiet day	
	22nd		Our trench mortars did good work on the Pairs and Argyll Crater groups. The enemy's retaliation was feeble	
	23rd		The Divisional artillery bombarded the enemy's area behind the support line at intervals during the day	
	24th		Quiet day Nothing to record	
	25th		Nothing to Report	

Army Form C. 2118

Instructions regarding War Diaries and Intelligence Summaries are contained in F. S. Regs., Part II. and the Staff Manual respectively. Title Pages will be prepared in manuscript.

WAR DIARY
or
INTELLIGENCE SUMMARY
(Erase heading not required.)

Place	Date	Hour	Summary of Events and Information	Remarks and references to Appendices
TRENCHES NEUVILLE ST VAAST	26		A raid on the enemy trenches was organized by 2/14th The London Regiment to take place at 12.10 a.m. The object of the raid was to cut off and capture the garrison of a Sap head. The enemy wire had been thoroughly reconnoitred and the raiding party got through an existing gap and entered the sap. On arrival at the sap head it was found to be empty so the party returned. See Appendix VIII.	Appendix VIII
			The relief of the battalion in firing line by those in Support and Reserve took place in the early morning without casualties	
	27		The Artillery carried out an organised bombardment behind the Hazel Group of Craters at 5.30 pm with apparent effect. Enemy Trench Mortars were active in the left Subsector	
	28th		A quiet day on the whole but towards evening the Enemy Trench Mortars were again active on the left. Weather very wet – Heavy Thunder storms	
	29th		Almost tropical rain fell during the day and night. Our artillery had arranged to bring up guns to cut enemy wire but the state of the ground prevented this being done	

1875 Wt. W593/826 1,000,000 4/15 J.B.C. & A. A.D.S.S./Forms/C. 2118.

Army Form C. 2118

Instructions regarding War Diaries and Intelligence Summaries are contained in F. S. Regs., Part II. and the Staff Manual respectively. Title Pages will be prepared in manuscript.

WAR DIARY
or
INTELLIGENCE SUMMARY
(Erase heading not required.)

Place	Date	Hour	Summary of Events and Information	Remarks and references to Appendices
TRENCHES NEUVILLE St VAAST	30th		The enemy artillery was rather more active. Our heavy guns fired a few rounds at SHEBAS BREASTS but no direct hits were scored. The long communication trenches which are necessary in this area were much damaged by the recent storms and much work will have to be done to them before the winter. The line being held so thinly it is difficult to find the working parties for the ordinary upkeep of the trenches.	
	31st		A quiet day. Nothing to record. All available men were engaged in repairing damage done to trenches by rain.	

LIST OF APPENDICES

Appendix	VI	Account of Raid by 2/13th Bn
"	VII	Account of the exploding of a mine under The PULPIT
"	VIII	Orders for raid by 2/14th Bn
"	IX	Casualties for month of August
"	X	Strength states of unit on 1st and 31st August
"	XI	Weekly intelligence Summaries

1875 Wt. W593/826 1,000,000 4/15 J.B.C. & A. A.D.S.S./Forms/C. 2118.

CONFIDENTIAL. N.I.1.4.

179th Infantry Brigade.

WEEKLY INTELLIGENCE SUMMARY.

For Week Ending August 8th. 1916.

GENERAL SUMMARY.

The past week has been more active generally, culminating in the Raid by the 2/13th London Regiment on the night of the 6th instant. Enemy T.M. Fire appears to be stronger opposite to our Left than our Right Sub-Sector. It was clearly noted on the night of the 6th that the Enemy put up a barrage of T.M. Fire in NO MAN'S LAND, making it very difficult for Raiding Party's return. Enemy M.G. indirect fire has not been so much in evidence as formerly. Our Patrols have been out nightly, whereas those of the Enemy have been infrequent and confined to covering the operations of Working Parties. Enemy has been very busy improving and strengthening his wire generally and again it has been noticed that he does not send up as many flares as formerly.

A spirit of nervousness appears to prevail in the Enemy Lines as at night he has been directing his fire - T.M's, Aerial Torpedoes, and Oil-Cans more on our SAPS and OBSERVATION LINES than on our FIRING and SUPPORT Lines, as if afraid of Raids.

The relief of the 2/15th and 2/16th Battalions L.R. took place on the 4th instant without any casualties.

Enemy Observation Balloons have been particularly active, as many as eight having been up at one time and all clearly visible from Brigade Headquarters. Enemy always heavily shell and also direct considerable M.G. Fire, on our Aeroplanes. Two Airships were observed flying very high. Particulars of the prisoners taken, Identity discs, etc. have been duly sent forward.

The Enemy appears to fire a Light T.M. from different CRATER points.

The following T.M's have been located at

A.16.a.90.01.

A.16.a.94.80.

SNIPERS POSTS: None definitely located.

SNIPERS BAGS: One Bomb Store blown up, two hits claimed.

Bde. H.Q.
August 9th 1916.

Sd. E W BAIRD
BRIGADIER GENERAL,
Comdg 179th Infantry Brigade.

W.I.R. 5.

179th Infantry Brigade.

WEEKLY INTELLIGENCE SUMMARY.

For week ending August 15th 1916.

GENERAL SUMMARY:

The chief item of the past week on our Front was the blowing of a Mine at 1[illegible].30 a.m. on the night of 10th and 11th August and the formation of the PULPIT CRATER, quite the largest individual one in this Sector. The near lip was occupied with little interference by the Enemy, some Machine Gun and Rifle Fire being directed at our Working and Consolidating Parties. No attempt as far as can be observed has been made by the Enemy to occupy the further or EASTERN Lip.

Generally greater activity has prevailed and the spirit of nervousness reported in last weekly review has if anything increased, the Enemy being more than ever alert for any movement on our part.

Our Artillery, T.M's and L.T.M's have done good work.

With regard to Lights, it has been observed that when the Enemy put up Flares which burst into two lights, this is apparently a signal for intensifying whatever kind of firing is in progress.

Our patrols report that Enemy activity is very slight, confining himself to Working Parties on his own immediate Front with at times covering parties a little further out. His energy has been considerable in strengthening his wire.

The Enemy appear to know our meal times as T.M's, Aerial Torpedoes and Oil-cans come over between 8 and 8.30 a.m. and 1 to 2 p.m.

Our Aerial activity has been considerable, the Enemy having expended much ammunition without doing our planes any serious damage.

The following have been located:-

T.M. at A.10.b.55.40., and alternative positions
at A.10.d.23.7 and 15

M.G. Emplacement at A.10.b.10.75,
and at A.10.b.50.30.

SAPHEAD at A.10.b.35.45.

SNIPERS BAG: 2 hits claimed.

Sd. EW Baird

BRIGADIER GENERAL,
Comdg 179th Infantry Brigade.

Bde.H.Q.
August 16th 1916.

CONFIDENTIAL. W.I.R. 6.

179th Infantry Brigade.

WEEKLY INTELLIGENCE SUMMARY.

For week ending August 22nd 1916.

GENERAL SUMMARY:

The Relief of the 2/15th and 2/16th Battalions London Regiment by the 2/13th and 2/14th Battalions London Regiment took place without casualties on the night of 19/20th August 1916.

This week has shewn considerable activity at times, more particularly from midday until past midnight, the mornings being generally quiet except about breakfast time, 8 - 8.30 a.m. when Aerial Torpedoes and Oilcans are sent over by the Enemy on our Firing Line.

Our T.M's, Medium and Light have done consistently good work and apart from damaging considerably Enemy Trenches and wire in various parts, one Enemy Bomb Store was hit and blown up.

Our new PULPIT CRATER, the consolidation of which has steadily continued, appears to cause the Enemy great uneasiness, as it is a constant daily target for T.M. Fire, Aerial Torpedoes and Snipers, and a nightly one for M. Guns in particular. The Enemy do not appear to be doing any work on their immediate side of this CRATER.

Our Artillery has straffed at various times particular sections of the Enemy Front and Support Lines.

Our Aerial activity has been considerable and much ammunition expended by the Enemy in unsuccessful attempts to thwart reconnaissance of their Lines. On an average two Enemy Aeroplanes per day endeavour to patrol over our lines.

Our Nightly Patrols in NO MAN'S LAND continue to report comparatively little Enemy activity in working parties and NIL in Patrols. Many of the CRATERS are unoccupied on Enemy Side during the day but have posts on them at night:

The following have been located:-

- T.M. at A.4.d.62.77.
- T.M. at A.16.a.97.80.
- T.M. at A.16.b.10.50.
- M.G. at A.16.c.73.95.
- SNIPERS POST at A.16.b.78.00.

SNIPERS' BAG: 7 hits claimed.

Sd BW BAIRD

Bde.H.Q.
August 23rd 1916.

BRIGADIER GENERAL,
Comdg 179th Infantry Brigade.

APPENDIX XI

CONFIDENTIAL.

179th Infantry Brigade.

W.I.R. 7.

WEEKLY INTELLIGENCE SUMMARY.

For week ending August 29th 1916.

GENERAL SUMMARY.

During the past week our Artillery activity has been maintained, the numerous intermittent bombardments having been successful in keeping under to a considerable extent Enemy Artillery activity, the latter, throughout the period under review, being extremely feeble in retaliation.

T.M's both Medium and Light have done sound work in conjunction with Artillery and Bombardments on their own, the Enemy Front and Support Lines suffering severely in places and one Iron Plate protected strong point (in particular) was demolished at A.10.b.25.80. Our M.G's have carried out systematic schemes of indirect fire, the hostile retaliation on some of our dumping points and C.T's showing, it is thought, that our Fire was successful.

Our Lewis Guns have been active in dispersing Working Parties.

The Relief of the 2/13th and 2/14th Battalions London Regiment by the 2/15th and 2/16th Battalions London Regiment took place in the early morning of the 26th instant without casualties.

Enemy activity has been principally confined to T.M's, Aerial Torpedoes and Rifle Grenades, the latter appearing now to have a somewhat increased range, some bursting well behind our Support Lines. The AUX RIETZ Corner has been a favourite hostile objective and the PULPIT CRATER has been singled out for attention from 5.9's registering, Oiling Bombs and Aerial Torpedoes.

Patrols have been out nightly, a good knowledge of NO MAN'S LAND and the strong and weak points in Enemy Wire, opposite our Front, as well as the CRATER Lips occupied by Enemy by day, and those by night, has now been obtained.

The weather has not on the whole been good for observation.

Our Snipers' Posts have been examined by the Divisional Officer and two new ones are in Course of construction in STONE STREET and GUILLERMOT.

Upwards of 400 yards of wiring has been erected on our Front.

An old French Trench connecting VERTHELLO and RIETZ is being reopened for Stretcher Bearer Traffic.

The following have been located;-

T.M. at A.16.b.05.65.
" " A.4.d.50.20.
" " A.4.d.50.50.
" " A.10.b.30.37.
O.P. at A.16.c.30.88.
SNIPERS' POST at A.16.a.75.10.

SNIPERS' BAGS: None claimed.

Sd. E W Band

Bde.H.Q.
August 30th 1916.

BRIGADIER GENERAL,
Comdg. 179th Infantry Brigade.

Appendix VI

Headquarters,
60th (London) Division.

I have to report that the Raid arranged to take place at 10.30 p.m. last night was carried out with the following results:-

The Medium T.M's. opened fire at 10.28, the Guns and Light T.M's at 10.30.

The Infantry debouched from the Sap close to the PULPIT at 10.33 p.m. and were reported all out at 10.34 p.m.

The man carrying the tape fell into a shell-hole and the tape became tangled in the reel of the man's pack. Thm

The raiding party pushed on and found the wire well out. They entered the enemy Trench without a casualty but found it very badly damaged and empty. It was also apparently blocked with the purpose of preventing the Raiding Party proceeding up it.

When Lieut. Read became aware of the situation he gave the signal to retire which was heard and answered to, all the men of the raiding party being counted out by him including one wounded man who wash brought away on one of the ladders.

The enemy was at this time putting an intense barrage between his lines and the PULPIT and it is reported that the party split up, some going to the left under Lieut. Stockwell. This party it appears mistook the German Trench for our own and it is when they jumped into this Trench that Corporal Wills secured his prisoner whom he brought into our Lines single-handed.

His arrival was reported to this Office at 11.25. It was not until 11.38 that a report came in stating that another 20 men had come in.

At 11.58 a report was received that all were out and were coming home in different directions.

On receipt of this message the signal was given to the Artillery to stop firing.

It is known that Lieut. Read was wounded in the arm and was last seen close to the point of entry. Nothing has been heard of Lieut. Stockwell since he started to lead his men round by the Left.

Patrols were sent out to search No-Man's Land but no trace of either of the missing Officers or men could be found.

At daylight four men came in by the Right Co. They stated that they had completely lost their way in the dark and dust and had intended staying in a shelter all day but at dawn they got their bearings and crawled home through the grass.

Just as it was getting light a German Patrol approached Territorial Sap. The Sentry on the Bombing Post threw a Bomb into it, killing one man whose body was pulled into our Trench.

Another badly wounded German has just been brought in (10.25 a.m. 7th). He formed one of the same Patrol as the man who was killed.

Both prisoner and the dead man belong to the same Regiment the 184th.

It is with regret that I have to report that the two Officers and 12 men are still missing and that four men were killed who did not belong to the Raiding Party.

A full detailed account has not yet been received from O.C., 2/13th Battalion L.R. as the Raiders were sent back to Billets before they could all be questioned.

A further report will follow.

Sd. E.W. Baird

Bde.H.Q.
August 7th 1916.

BRIGADIER GENERAL,
Comdg 179th Infantry Brigade.

REPORT BY LIEUT. W. READ, 2/13th LONDON REGIMENT, 8/8/16.

I beg to report that at 10.33 p.m. last night my party left the PULPIT to raid the GERMAN TRENCHES as per Scheme previously submitted. On the way over, the tape got into difficulties owing to the explosion of a Trench Mortar and this tape was not laid all the way to the Bosche Lines as previously arranged.

On arriving at the German Trenches I found that although the wire defences had been broken down by the Trench Mortars, the Trench itself was barricaded. Seeing the state of affairs, and also not having the necessary implements to break down these heavy barricades, I gave the order to withdraw. A few men got into the Right Trench by crawling underneath the barricade and found no Germans there.

I saw all the men out of the Trenches and then gave orders to the covering party to withdraw, when a Trench Mortar wounded several of them and also the last Bombers to leave the Trenches. A hail of Trench Mortars then came over.

I found 3354 Pte. Pickard, G. wounded. I got hold of him and got him back to a shell hole, where I came across No.4362 Pte. Barham H.R. No. 5770 Pte. FIELD F. and 2887 Pte. SHARP.J.W. the latter slightly wounded.

Owing to the tape being destroyed, I was unable to find my way back and Ptes. Barham and Field reconnoitred for the purpose of finding the direction of our own Trenches. Ptes. Barham and Field took out the bolts of any Rifles they found. I came across one dead man whom I was unable to identify and bring along with me.

We then took refuge in a shell hole which turned out to be quite near EDINBURGH CRATER, and which I was unable to identify. We stayed there all day yesterday and regret to say that Pte. Pickard died about mid-day (7th). We were unable to bring him along, having already one wounded man and myself (broken wrist) so we left him there and have given particulars of his whereabouts to the Battalion.

We left the shell hole at approximately 9 p.m. yesterday to endeavour to find our own lines and we eventually met one of the Kensington Search parties at about 1.30 a.m. (8.8.16).

All men were counted out and I was the last to leave the German Lines.

I understand that No.2538 Cpl. Wills, R.O. secured one prisoner. This man was very plucky throughout the whole raid and I should like to bring his name to your notice. I would also bring to your notice the names of No. 4362 Pte. Barham, H.R., No.5770 Pte. Field.F. and No.2887 Pte. Sharp, J.W. who, under very trying circumstances, were very plucky.

(sd) W. READ.
Lieut.

8th August 1916.

179th Infantry Brigade.

SECRET.

Copy No. 4

OPERATION ORDER NO. 6.

APPENDIX VII

Ref: ROCLINCOURT
Sheet 51B. 1/10,000.
and attached Sketch.

1. A Mine will be exploded at A.4.d.2½.2, at a time to be notified later.

2. The following parties will be detailed to seize and consolidate the CRATER:-

(a) 1 Officer. 8 O.R. 2/13th Bn.L.R. including 2 Lewis Gunners with Gun & 6 Drums.	Rifle & Bayonet each 50 Rounds S.A.A. 10 Bombs in bucket " Slung Shovel " 4 Empty Sandbags " Bombing Shield "
(b) 1 Officer & 3 R.E. 12 O.R. 2/13th Bn.L.R.	Rifle & Bayonet 50 Rounds S.A.A. each. 3 Picks remainder shovel " 6 Loop-hole plates. 50 Sandbags (empty) 2 pairs Wire Cutters. 2 pairs Hedging Gloves.
(b.1) 1 Officer, 8 O.R. 2/13th Bn.L.R.	Rifle & Bayonet 50 Rounds S.A.A., each. Pick & Shovel "
(c) 1 R.E. 10 O.R. 2/13th Bn.L.R.	4 Rolls French Wire. 2 half-rolls Barbed Wire. 12 Iron Picquets. 2 large screw picquets. 2 small mallets. 2 knife rests. 4 pairs Hedging Gloves. 6 pairs Wire Cutters.
(d) 8 O.R. 2/13th Bn.L.R.	Rifle & Bayonet 50 Rounds S.A.A., each. 1 Pick and 1 Shovel "
(e) 1 R.E. and 10 O.R. 2/13th Bn.L.R.	Same as (c) plus 12 Pit props for Bombing Post.

(f) Reserve in Dug-outs: 1 Officer & 20 O.R. 2/13th Bn.L.R.

3. Duties of Parties:-

(a) Seizing Party.

Starting Point: Point 4. on Sketch Map.
Time: x.
Objective: Far lip of Crater.
General Instructions: The Officer Commanding this party will reconnoitre from Point 4. to a spot where the near lip of Crater will probably be. He will lay a tape and mark the Line with sticks with white tops.

Directly the Mine is blown he will lead his party to the far lip and distribute his men along it from Point 1 to Point 3, as shewn by dotted line where he will remain until he receives orders to retire from O.C. Consolidating Party.

(b) & (b.1). Consolidating Party.

Starting Point: Point 4.
Time: Follow party A.
Objective: Near lip of Crater.
General Instructions:

(b) will be divided into 3 parties of 4 each.
Right Party will construct Sniping Post at Point 3.
Centre Party " " Bombing Post at Point 2.
Left Party " " Sniping Post at Point 1.

(b.1). will construct Communication Trench between Points 2 and 3 and will furnish 2 men to act as connecting files with Party (a).

(c) Right Wiring Party:
This party will remain in Dug-Outs at top of GUILLERMOT until ordered to move when they will proceed to Point 4. and collect their Stores. They will then proceed to a point 5 yds. E. of Point 3 and erect an obstacle as shewn on sketch.

(d) Clearing Party:
Starting Point: Point 8.
Time: x.
Objective: WHITAKER'S CUTTING at Point 6.
General Instructions. The Party will divide into 2 parties of 4. Right Party will clear WHITAKER'S CUTTING between Point 6 and 7 and afterwards to dig new Trench from Point 7 to Point 2. Left Party to clear Trench from Point 6 to PULPIT.

(e) Left Wiring Party:
This party will remain in Dug-Outs at top of STOKE STREET until ordered to move when they will proceed to left arm of WHITAKER'S CUTTING at Point 5 and collect their Stores. They will then proceed to a point 5 yards E. of Point 1 and erect an Obstacle as shewn on Sketch.

(f) Reserve Party:
This party will be divided into two of 10 each. Right Reserve Party will remain in Dug-Outs at top of GUILLERMOT and Left Reserve Party in Dug-Outs at top of STOKE STREET where they will await orders.
50 Bombs will be drawn by each Party from their respective Company Bomb Stores.

4. The necessary Stores will be dumped at STOKE STREET during daylight on the 9th instant. When it is known on what date the Mine is to be blown these Stores will be taken up and placed in the positions from which they will have to be carried to Crater. This will be done as soon as it is dark on the night on which it is arranged that the Mine should be blown.
The Stores for Right Wiring Party at A.4.d.1½.½ (near No. 9 Post).
The Stores for Left Wiring Party in left arm of WHITAKER'S CUTTING A.4.d.2.2½.
Whilst the right parties Stores are being placed in position a Covering Party of 6 O.R. will remain in Observation and will not withdraw until they get orders from O.C. Seizing Party.

5. Stretcher Bearers. 8 Stretcher Bearers will be on duty at D. Coy Headquarters.

6. Artillery and Trench Mortars will co-operate. Scheme attached.

7. Watches will be synchronized at 179th Brigade Headquarters at an hour which will be notified by wire numbered B.M.500.
The following will send representatives:-
O.C. Central Group R.A.
O.C. 2/13th Battalion L.R.
O.C. 2/4th Field Co.R.E.
O.C. 175th Tunnelling Co. R.E.
O.C. 60x Medium Trench Mortar Battery.
O.C. 179th Light Trench Mortar Battery.

W.N.HERBERT.
Major,
BRIGADE MAJOR,
179th Infantry Brigade.

Copy Nos. 1 & 2. File.
" " 3 & 4. 2/13th Bn.L.R.
" " 5. O.C.Central Group R.A.
" " 6. 175th Tunnelling Co.R.E.
" " 7. 60x. M.T.M. Battery.
Copy No.8. 179th L.T.M.Battery.
" " 9. 2/4th Field Co.R.E.
Copy No.10.
" " 11.
Copy No.12.

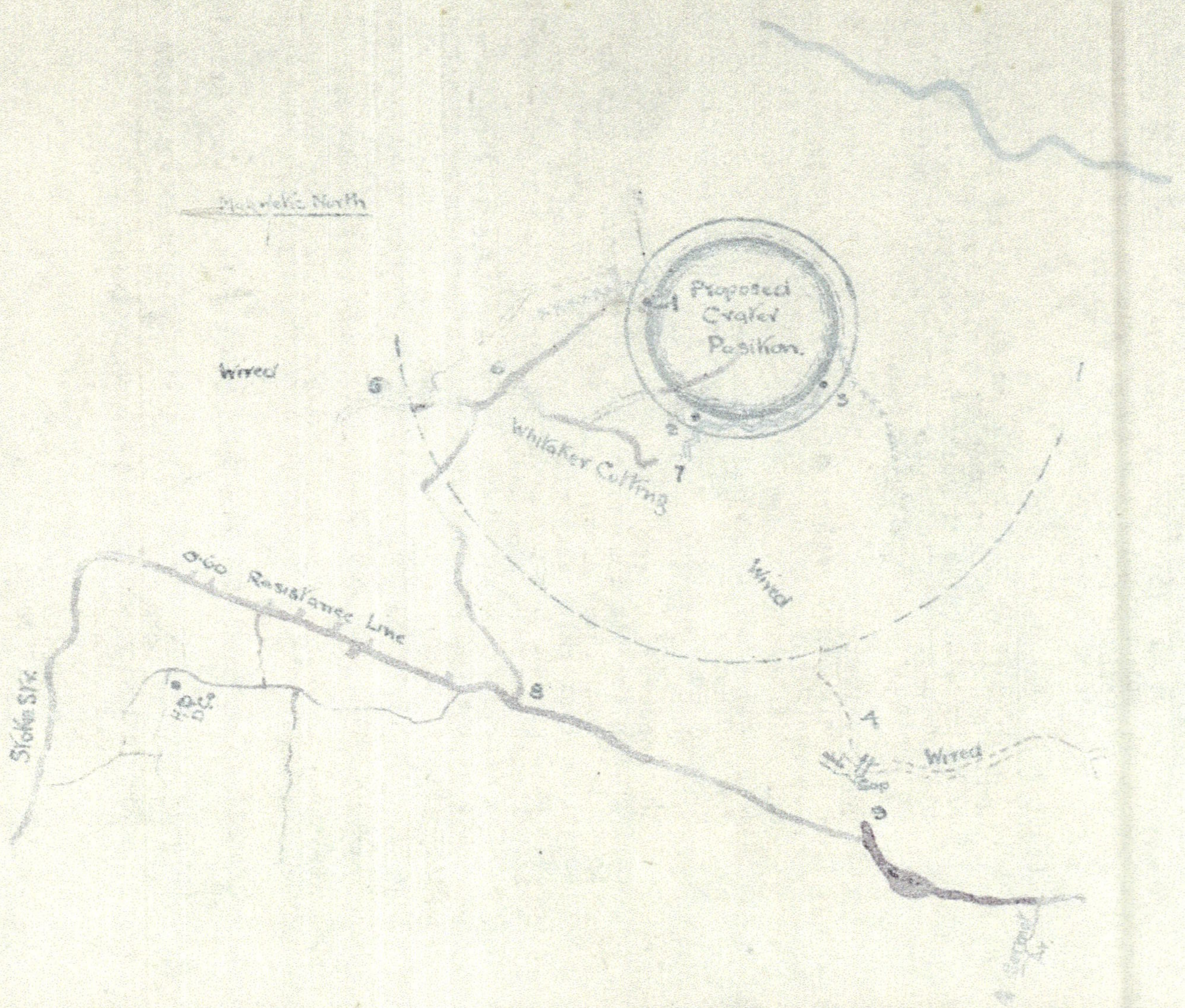

Magnetic North
Proposed
Crater
Position.
Wired
Whitaker Cutting
Wired
Resistance Line
Wired
Stoke St.

Trench Mortar Programme.

	No. of guns.	Target.		Rate.	Time.
1.60 M.T.M.B.	2.	Enemy front line.	A 4 d 4.6 to A 4 d 1.9½	Rapid.	X to X + 5.
				Slow	X 5 to X 30
	1.	Trenches	A 10 b 4.6 to A 10 b 3.½	Rapid.	X to X 5.
				Slow	X 5 to X 30
179 L.T.M.B.	2.	Trenches	A 4 d 5.5 and A 10 a 4.8 }	Rapid.	X to X 2.
	2.	Trenches	A 10 b 3.9½ to A 10 b 4.5 {	Slow.	X 2 to X 30

After X 30 T.M's will fire at any suitable target and endeavour to silence enemy T.M's.

ARTILLERY PROGRAMME.

Feint. The following bombardment will commence at X in order to distract attention.

X to X 5	Shrapnel	Section Fire	10 seconds	From A 10 c.9.0.1	to A 10 c.99.3.
X 5 to X 10	H.E.	" "	20 "	" "	"
Howitzer	H.E.	" "	20 "	" "	"

Fire. If called upon to fire only.

A to X 10 — 1 Section blocks Front line about A 4 d 4.8.
" " — 1 Section " " " " A 10 b 4.9.
1 Battery searches 2nd line with shrapnell from A 10 b 6.95 to A 10 d 65.5.
X 10 onwards. 1 Section Howitzer A 4 d 35.60.
" " A 10 b 60.70
1 " 18 Pdrs. A 4 d 4.85.
1 " " A 4 d 25.80 to A 4 d 65.36
1 Battery " A 4 d 65.36 to A 4 d 65.07
1 Section " A 4 d 65.07 to A 10 b 60.95
1 " " Block Front line A 10 b 35.98.

N.B. It has been decided that no artillery or Mortar Fire will be opened until required. If the trench mortars are required the following signal will be sent up from D coys Headquarters. A volley of 4 Very Lights fired in a westerly direction. On this signal the bombardment scheduled to begin at X will open.

If the Artillery are required a message will be sent by telephone direct from F.O.O. who will be in touch with O.C. A/13th Battalion L.R. at D Coy H.Q.

Headquarters,
179th Infantry Brigade. 11th August 1916.

I beg to submit the following report on Operations which took place night of 10/11th August 1916.

The object was to seize CRATER which would be formed by Mine Explosion at 12.30 a.m. 11/8/16.

By 12.15 a.m. all parties and Stores were in readiness at their allotted positions.

The Mine was blown punctually at 12.30 a.m. All was quiet after the explosion, and there was no firing. I ordered the wiring parties out at 12.35 a.m. The first Enemy Machine Guns were heard shortly before 1 a.m. By 12.49 a.m. I received a message that the CRATER was taken and consolidation was in progress. At 1 a.m. I heard that Lieut. KILLINGBACK, R.E. was wounded and I sent a message to Lieut. THOMPSON, 2/15th L.R. that he was to assume command.

At 1.16 a.m. it was reported that one of the Sniper's Posts was finished. Great difficulty was experienced in digging a Communication Trench on slope of CRATER, as the earth was so loose that it fell in almost as soon as it was shovelled out. I suggest employment of some quick form of revetment for this kind of work. Between 1.23 a.m. and 1.41 a.m. great difficulty was experienced by the left Wiring Party as they were badly sniped. It was with this party that two Sappers were killed so I withdrew the party at 1.41 a.m.

At 1.28 a.m. I regret to say that I received a message that Lieut. KILLINGBACK, R.E. was killed.

At 1.40 a.m. I had to order up ten men extra to help in the digging as work was progressing slowly and we would not otherwise have been able to finish consolidation by daylight.

Work was now proceeding slowly. Great difficulty was experienced in clearing WHITAKER's CUTTING and digging a Communication Trench to CRATER as the cleared Trench was filled in again by Trench Mortars.

About 3 a.m. the Working Party were beginning to feel very tired and five men fainted at work. At 3.30 a.m. I managed to collect 10 more men for work and I now decided that the work would be far enough advanced to enable me to hold the CRATER by daylight. This decision was confirmed when I inspected the work in progress shortly afterwards.

By 4.50 a.m. all working parties were withdrawn and the Bombers Post garrisoned.

There are one or two points which may be of use in future. The line from starting point to probable position of CRATER was well-marked beforehand by tape and short pickets with bunches of paper tied on top. The tape was cut in 4 places so that it could not be blown away at an angle and thus mislead the parties. It was reported that the right direction could not have been kept without the tape, owing to smoke and dust.

The looseness of the ground on slope of CRATER was another difficulty and hasty revetments are suggested.

It is essential that each party should either carry their own stores to or see them at the Starting Point, otherwise confusion is bound to be the result.

The ground over which parties have to go should be very carefully reconnoitred by those in charge previously.

Altogether 86 men of this Battalion were employed under supervision of R.E.

I should like to express my admiration of the way in which the 2/4th London Field Co. R.E. who were in charge of my parties worked, and my regret at the unfortunate losses sustained by them.

I should specially like to bring before your notice the conduct of Corporal Gordon, R.E. This N.C.O. undertook supervision of R.E. work on the death of Lieut. KILLINGBACK. He moved from party to party under snipers' fire and carried out his duty in a most efficient manner. He constantly reported to me thus rendering great assistance.

Lieut. G.V.THOMPSON took command of all the parties when Lieut. KILLINGBACK was killed and proved most efficient.

2/Lieut. L. G. GATES was in command of the Seising Party and did all that was required.

(sd) G.H.MACKENZIE.

Lieut-Colonel,
Comdg. 2/13th Battalion London
Regiment.

COPY.

SECRET.
O.P.8

A Raid is being made by the 179th Infantry Brigade on the night of Friday August 25th at an hour to be notified hereafter.
They hope to accomplish their object without any Artillery Bombardment, but if called on the Batteries below will form a barrage.

A/300 A 16 c 8.9 to A 16 c 97.95

C/301 A 16 c 97.95 to A 16 a 95.17

B/302 A 16 a 95.17 to A 16 a 91.23

D/302 T.M.Emplacement A 16 c 9.7 and Front Trench A 16 a 91.23

B and D/302 will use H.E.

A/300 and C/301 will use Shrapnel.

If called on fire will be opened by 18pr Batteries at Section fire 10 secs. Howitzer at Section fire 20 secs.
Other details will be arranged later.
Acknowledge under name JINGLE.

(Sgd) H.M.Drake
Lt Col R.F.A
Comdg Centre Group.

23/8/16

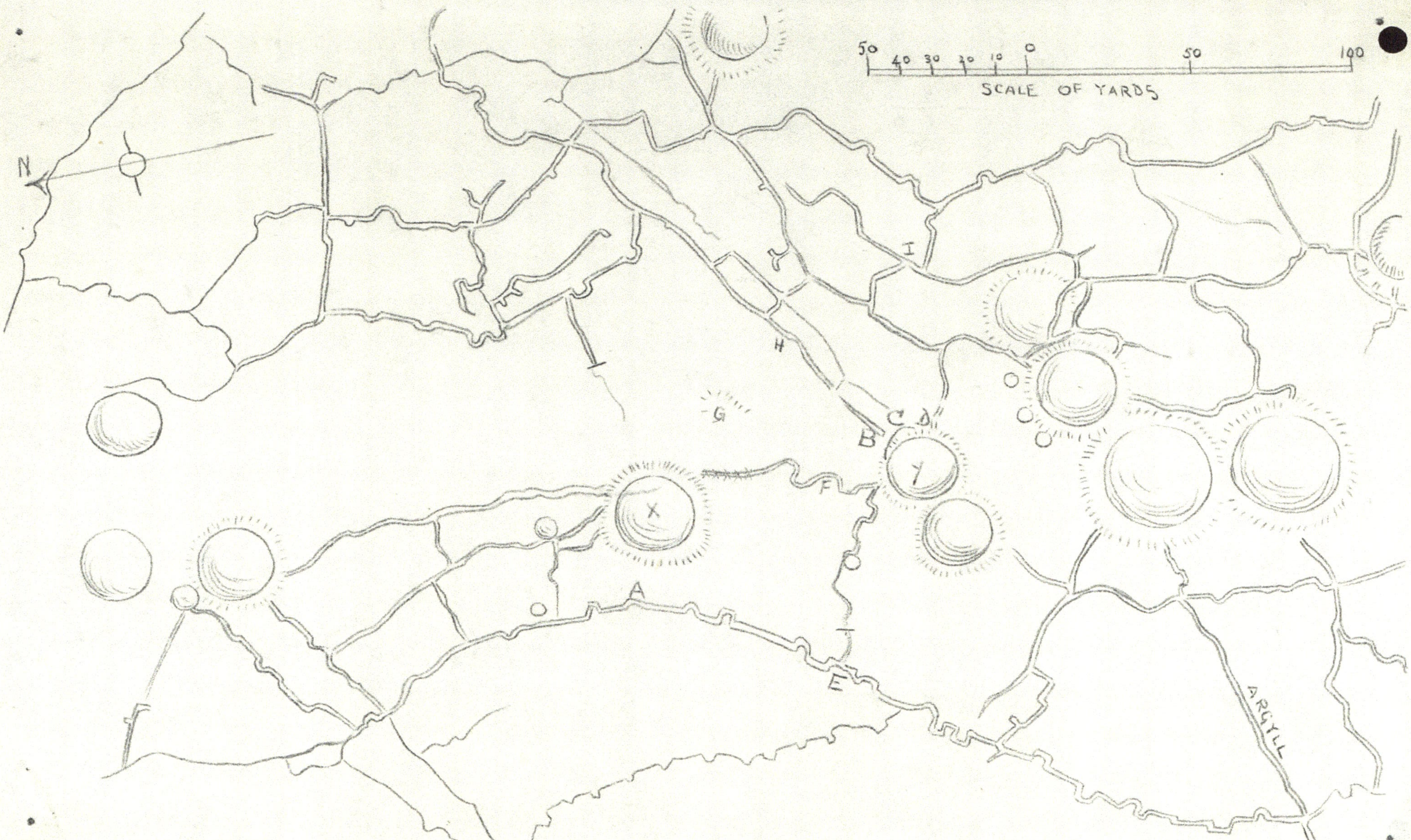
50 40 30 20 10 0 50 100
SCALE OF YARDS
N
ARGYLL
A
B
C
D
E
F
G
H
I
X
Y

APPENDIX VIII

SECRET.

Raid by 2/14th Battalion London Regiment.

at.....12.10 am.... 26th August 1916.

under Lt. T.D.C.MACLAGAN. 2nd in Command 2/Lt. C.H.GOSSIP.

REFERENCE.

Map. ROCLINCOURT. Sheet 51B NW1
and Sketch Map.

---

1. OBJECT. To obtain identification.

2. <u>The party consists of 4 groups</u>

(1) Crater Guard.	1 N.C.O. 1 Bayonet Man. 2 Bombers.
(2) Supporting Party.	1 Officer (2nd in Command) 1 N.C.O. 2 Bayonet Men. 1 Bomber.
(3) Covering Party.	1 N.C.O. 3 Men.
(4) Raiding Party.	Lt. T.D.C.MACLAGAN. 2 N.C.Os 4 Bombers.

3. <u>DUTIES OF GROUPS.</u>

Groups will go out in the above order.
No1 will go out from Point A on Sketch and take up a position guarding the Saps N of Crater X as it is known that small enemy patrols have used these Saps at night.

No 2 will go out from Point A keeping to south of Crater X and take up a position at F in Sap joining Craters X and Y where they will wait in readiness to assist raiding party if required.

No 3 will go out from Point A, cross Crater X to point G in some bushes. They will lay a Tape to this point as they go out. Their duty is to cover the left of the Raiding Party and they will remain there until the Raiding Party has returned.

No 4 will follow the Tape from A to G, gain touch with Party at G and move on to Point H where they will enter the Sap. They will then proceed up Sap towards points B and C and endeavour to take Sentry Group by surprise. They will return with their Prisoners round N lip of Crater Y to point F and so back to point A.

4. <u>COMMUNICATIONS.</u>
2nd. Lt TOCHER will be on duty at point A to which a wire will be laid from Right Company Headquarters at Junction of RAWSON STREET and VICTOIRE. He will be responsible for calling up the Artillery if required.

On return of the Raiding Party (No 4) 3 Green Rockets will be sent up from point A as a signal for the remaining parties to withdraw.

If the Artillery have opened fire 3 White Cluster Rockets will be fired when the whole party have returned as a signal to cease fire.

2nd. Lt TOCHER will be responsible for both these Rocket Signals.

5. <u>ARTILLERY.</u>
The Artillery will be standing by to open barrage fire as shewn in attached schedule from 12.10a.m. If they are not called upon a telephone message will be sent from point A when the parties have returned.

6. STOKES GUNS.

179th L.T.M.B. will co-operate with the Artillery in forming a barrage if required. In addition to this 1 Gun will fire occasional shots on Point J commencing at.................. This is in order to help the Raiding Party keep direction.

7. SPECIAL ARRANGEMENTS.

(1) Pass Word................. answered by.................

(2) Code Word for withdrawal...............................

(3) All papers and documents to be left behind. Orders, in case of being taken prisoner, to be read over before starting.

(4) Faces, Hands and Bayonets to be darkened.

(5) A Dug-out prepared ready for return.

(6) Medical Aid Post prepared in Firing Line.

(7) Extra Stretcher Bearers on duty.

(8) Open Sentry Posts.

8. GENERAL.

It is the intention to carry out the Raid by stealth and, if possible, without Artillery Fire.
All parties except Raiding Party are to be in position by...... .... when the Raiding Party will move out.
Should these Parties be discovered and fired upon before the Raiding Party has left, the O.C. Raiding Party will decide as to action to be taken.
If on the other hand the Raiding Party has gone out the Officer in charge at point A will decide as to whether the Artillery barrage should be opened.

APPENDIX IX

179th Infantry Brigade.

CASUALTIES FOR THE MONTH OF AUGUST 1916.

UNIT.	KILLED.	WOUNDED.	MISSING.	TOTAL.
2/13th Battalion London Regiment.	25.	x25.	8.	58.
2/14th " " "	1.	26.	-	27.
2/15th " " "	5.	x17.	-	22.
2/16th " " "	10.	46.	-	56.
179th Machine Gun Co.	1.	1.	-	2.
179th Light Trench Mortar Battery.	-	4.	-	4.
60x Medium Trench Mortar Battery.	-	-	-	-
	42.	119.	8.	169.

x Includes 2 Accidental.

N.B. This does not include the Officers' casualties shewn below:-

OFFICERS WOUNDED.

2/13th Battalion London Regiment:- Lieut. W. Read.

2/14th Battalion " " Lieut-Colonel R. Dunsmore.
Lieut. C. Wallis.
2/Lieut. S.G. Wilson.

2/16th Battalion " " 2/Lieut. E.B. Brown.

OFFICERS MISSING.

2/13th Battalion London Regiment:- 2/Lieut. F. R. Stockwell.

APPENDIX V

179th Infantry Brigade.

STRENGTH RETURN.

As at AUGUST 1ST. 1916.

UNIT.	OFFICERS.	OTHER RANKS.
179th Infantry Brigade Headquarters:	12.	49.
2/13th Battalion London Regiment:	30.	926.
2/14th Battalion London Regiment:	38.	948.
2/15th Battalion London Regiment.	32.	944.
2/16th Battalion London Regiment.	31.	964.
179th Machine Gun Co.	10.	141.
179th Light Trench Mortar Battery:	4.	46.
60x Medium Trench Mortar Battery.	1.	23.
	158.	4041.

This Return includes Officers, N.C.Os. and Other Ranks attached from other Units.

Appendix X

179th Infantry Brigade.

STRENGTH RETURN.

As at AUGUST 31ST. 1916.

UNIT.	OFFICERS.	OTHER RANKS.
179th Infantry Brigade Headquarters	12.	52.
2/13th Battalion London Regiment.	29.	919.
2/14th Battalion London Regiment.	40.	939.
2/15th Battalion London Regiment.	41.	926.
2/16th Battalion London Regiment.	35.	988.
179th Machine Gun Co.	10.	144.
179th Light Trench Mortar Battery.	4.	46.
60x Medium Trench Mortar Battery.	2.	23.
	173.	4037.

This Return includes Officers, N.C.Os. and Other Ranks attached from other Units.

Vol. IV

Confidential.

WAR DIARY

Vol 4

179th Inf. Bde.

From 1st Sept. 1916

To 30th Sept. 1916.

Instructions regarding War Diaries and Intelligence Summaries are contained in F. S. Regs., Part II. and the Staff Manual respectively. Title Pages will be prepared in manuscript.

WAR DIARY
or
~~INTELLIGENCE SUMMARY~~
(Erase heading not required.)

179th Infantry Brigade
September 1916
VOL 4

Army Form C. 2118

Place	Date	Hour	Summary of Events and Information	Remarks and references to Appendices
NEUVILLE ST VAAST TRENCHES	1.		The battalion in the line was relieved by battalion in support and reserve in the early hours of the morning without casualties. RICHARDS Battery fired 10 heavy shells on SHEBAS BREASTS at 3.15 pm. No direct hit was obtained but damage to material in vicinity was done.	[illegible]
	2.		Our Artillery and T.Ms cut the wire in front of Enemy front line in several places. This operation was however much hindered by heavy rain. Enemy T.Ms retaliated and much damage was done to PARIS REDOUBT	[illegible]
	3.		A quiet day. Nothing to record	[illegible]
	4.		Enemy was very quiet all day. Our M.T.Ms. cut some more wire in front of Enemy line	[illegible]
	5.		A quiet day. Nothing of importance to record	[illegible]
	6.		The Divisional Artillery bombarded the enemy communication trenches intermittently throughout the day, during which there was considerable	

Instructions regarding War Diaries and Intelligence Summaries are contained in F. S. Regs., Part II. and the Staff Manual respectively. Title Pages will be prepared in manuscript.

WAR DIARY
or
INTELLIGENCE SUMMARY
(Erase heading not required.)

Army Form C. [illegible]8

Place	Date	Hour	Summary of Events and Information	Remarks and references to Appendices
TRENCHES NEUVILLE ST VAAST	6th (con)		Aerial Activity The enemy exploded a mine near our CLAUDOT Sap at 9.55pm which formed a small crater adjoining the old one. About 7 minutes after the mine was blown the enemy put a barrage on our trenches behind it, which caused a few casualties. One man only was killed by the explosion of the mine although 1 post was practically destroyed.	
	7th		The crater formed by the mine on 6th was placed in a state of defence during the night the CLAUDOT Sap being joined with the MERPILLAT Sap by the opening of an old trench. As the enemy was suspected of tamping and loading a mine in the PHILIP Group it was decided to blow a mine, which was already laid, to destroy his gallery. A long low crater was formed but it was not thought worth while consolidating it. It is doubtful if the enemy's gallery was damaged. Miners are going down to listen for signs of his continuing work.	
	8th		No definite signs of work continuing in enemy gallery. This was a very quiet day and much work was done on new post at CLAUDOT	

Army Form C. [illegible]8

Instructions regarding War Diaries and Intelligence Summaries are contained in F. S. Regs., Part II. and the Staff Manual respectively. Title Pages will be prepared in manuscript.

WAR DIARY
or
INTELLIGENCE SUMMARY
(Erase heading not required.)

Place	Date	Hour	Summary of Events and Information	Remarks and references to Appendices
TRENCHES NEUVILLE ST VAAST	9th		Rather more firing on Enemy's part both with guns and T.Ms. otherwise nothing to record.	[illegible]
	10th		A quiet day nothing of importance to record	[illegible]
	11th		At 3.0 am 2/15th Bn London Regt carried out a successful raid on the enemy trenches opposite the PARIS REDOUBT. Four prisoners were captured and several dugouts bombed. The account of the Raid is shown in appendix. The Division transferred from 3rd to 1st Army from 12 midnight 11th/12th.	APPENDIX XII [illegible]
	12th		A quiet day nothing to record	[illegible]
	13th		Battalions in Support and Reserve relieved battalions in the line during the early hours of the morning without casualty.	[illegible]
	14th		Our guns and Medium Trench Mortars were employed in cutting the Enemy's wire in front of firing line and support trenches opposite the FROGES Sap, otherwise there was very little activity. The Stokes guns & Lewis guns cooperated with patrols at night to prevent the enemy mending the gaps which were cut.	[illegible]

1875 Wt. W593/826 1,000,000 4/15 J.B.C. & A. A.D.S.S./Forms/C. 2118.

Instructions regarding War Diaries and Intelligence Summaries are contained in F. S. Regs., Part II. and the Staff Manual respectively. Title Pages will be prepared in manuscript.

WAR DIARY
or
INTELLIGENCE SUMMARY
(Erase heading not required.)

Army Form C. 2118

Place	Date	Hour	Summary of Events and Information	Remarks and references to Appendices
TRENCHES NEUVILLE St-VAAST	15.		Wire cutting was continued the gaps made on the previous day being widened. Otherwise nothing to record	DHH
	16.		The Enemy Trench Mortars were rather more active than usual. Especially on extreme left.	DHH
	17.		Quiet day. 1st Bn Dorset Regiment arrived in ECOIVRES. Two companies ordered to be accomodated in 179 I.B. advance area. Advance parties arrived at 8.0pm	DHH
	18th		A very wet day. Both Artillery work and work on trenches much impeded. Many of the trenches considerably damaged by old sandbags bursting and the sandbags from the mines which had been piled on the sides of the trenches slipping in.	DHH
	19th		The Battalions in firing line were relieved in the early morning by battalions in Support and Reserve without casualty. A fine day but a very wet night	DHH

Instructions regarding War Diaries and Intelligence Summaries are contained in F. S. Regs., Part II. and the Staff Manual respectively. Title Pages will be prepared in manuscript.

WAR DIARY
or
INTELLIGENCE SUMMARY
(Erase heading not required.)

Army Form C. 2118

Place	Date	Hour	Summary of Events and Information	Remarks and references to Appendices
TRENCHES NEUVILLE ST. VAAST	20		Much damage done during the night by heavy rain. The work during the day was confined to clearing the trenches	[illegible]
	21		A quiet day nothing to record	[illegible]
	22.		Some smoke clouds were observed coming from the enemy's line at an altitude of 200 feet. These were reported to be poison clouds, but no ill effect was felt. The "Gas alert" was ordered	[illegible]
	23.		A quiet day. At 11.0 pm. the 2/16th Bn carried out a successful raid on the enemy trenches. see Appendix XIII Five prisoners were taken.	Appendix XIII [illegible]
	24th		A quiet day. A new type of aerial torpedo which the enemy had been using for some days was picked up in an undamaged condition. Its weight is about 20 lbs. and is evidently fired from a mortar of about 4 inch calibre. The specimen was forwarded to the Division	[illegible]
	25th		The Bns in support and Reserve relieved the Bns in the line without casualty. A very quiet day	[illegible]

Instructions regarding War Diaries and Intelligence Summaries are contained in F. S. Regs., Part II. and the Staff Manual respectively. Title Pages will be prepared in manuscript.

WAR DIARY
or
INTELLIGENCE SUMMARY
(Erase heading not required.)

Army Form C. 2118

Place	Date	Hour	Summary of Events and Information	Remarks and references to Appendices
NEUVILLE ST VAAST TRENCHES	26		The G.O.C. XVII Corps presented medals to men of Division including 3 men of 2/15th Bn London Regt on parade at BRAY. The 2/15th Bn London Regiment which was in rest and details of the battalions of the other two brigades were on parade. After the parade a demonstration of a Smoke attack and FLAMMENWERFER	W.H.H.
	27		A relief was suspected to have taken place last night as much more activity both of rifle and T.M.s was apparent during the day. Enemy T.M.s were very active between 7 and 11 pm.	W.H.H.
	28.		Nothing to record	W.H.H.
	29		Enemy T.Ms active. A new listening apparatus capable of picking up messages at a radius of 2000 yards was installed on our front	W.H.H.
	30th		At 2.45 am 2/14th Bn London Regt carried out a successful raid on Enemy Trenches capturing 5 prisoners of 107 Regt. See Appendix XIV	Appendix XIV W.H.H.

1875 Wt. W593/826 1,000,000 4/15 J.B.C. & A. A.D.S.S./Forms/C. 2118.

Instructions regarding War Diaries and Intelligence Summaries are contained in F. S. Regs., Part II. and the Staff Manual respectively. Title Pages will be prepared in manuscript.

WAR DIARY
or
INTELLIGENCE SUMMARY
(Erase heading not required.)

179 I.B.

September 1916

Army Form C. 2118

Place	Date	Hour	Summary of Events and Information	Remarks and references to Appendices
			List of Appendices.	
			XII Account of RAID by 2/15th Bn London Regt.	
			XIII " " " " 2/16th " " "	
			XIV " " " " 2/14th " " "	
			XV Casualties for month of September	
			XVI Stringth State for 1st and 30th of month	
			XVII Weekly Intelligence Reports	
			W.H.	

Appendix XII

To G.O.C., 179th Infantry Brigade.

REPORT on RAID. 10/11th September 1916.

In accordance with Raid Operation Orders already forwarded our Raid on the German Trenches was successfully carried out this morning at 3 a.m.

The party left our Lines at 2.45 a.m. and were all back at 3.30 a.m.

Casualties: 2 Officers wounded.
4 men wounded of whom one has since died.

Prisoners: Four prisoners were taken, of whom one was severely wounded.
All prismners belonged to the 184th Regt. The unwounded prisoners were at once despatched to Advance Brigade Headquarters.

Conduct: Officers. I cannot speak too highly of the work performed by Lieut. Peatfield, and 2nd Lieut. Thompson in organising and carrying out the Raid. They had forgotten no detail, had the full confidence of their men and behaved throughout with coolness and gallantry. I hope that they may be considered for special recognition.

Conduct: O. R. Non-Commissioned Officers and men all did well and showed great keenmsse both during training and in the actual operationz. I hope that the following may be considered for reward or mention:-

Corporal Jones.
Sergt. Quinton.
Corporal Marshall.
Pte.
Pte.

State of Enemy Trenches etc. As both Officers are wounded it is not possible to obtain a good account of the German Trenches, but it appears that at the point entered, the Trenches are very wide (12 feet ?) and deep.
The morale of the Enemy was low and the only opposition encountered was from Bombing Parties in two small Trenches immediately E. of Point of entry and which we had originally intended to include in our Raid.

Artillery. (a) Our own artillery fire was most accurate and effective and completely covered our withdrawal.
(b) The Enemy's Artillery was feeble and badly directed. They placed a barrage on the ELBE and CLAUDOT Trenches but caused no casualties.

Methods. All plans and methods for carrying out and facilitating the raid worked well and the two which were perhaps most useful were:-

(1) Paper chase trail.
(2) Decoy guiding Lanterns.

These latter were put up on Posts 60 yards apart and about 500 yards N. of our point of re-entry to our own line. Much of the Enemy Artillery and Torpedo Fire was directed on these lanterns.

Medical arrangements. Owing to lack of suitable Dug-out accommodation, it was impossible to establish an aid post in front line, but a party of bearers were at the point of re-entry and no difficulty was experienced in dealing with casualties.

Subsequent. Since the return of our party several small parties of Germans have been noticed in NO MAN'S LAND evidently trying to find their missing men or to pick up the trail of our party. Two of the enemy approached one of our posts at about 4. a.m. and were unfortunately bombed instead of being shot by the men on duty.

Further details. Any further details which may be received will be forwarded in an additional report.

Officers' reports. I attach statements made to me by Lieuts. Peatfield and Thompson, and there is no doubt that these statements can be amplified later.

Co-operation. The Co-operation of Trench Mortars and Stokes Guns and Machine Guns was most valuable, especially the latter, which enabled us to stop enemy wiring parties and protected our flanks on a part of the ground which the artillery could not deal with.

(sd) G. de PUTRON.
Lieut-Col.
Comdg. 2/15th Battn.London Regt.

11/9/1916.

STATEMENT BY LIEUT. B. PEATFIELD.

The night previous to the raid was quiet. A German Working Party of approximately five men had been heard from 10 p.m. to midnight at work on the wire. Lewis Gun Fire was brought to bear on this party but their work was continued inside the German Trenches.

At 2.15 a.m. Lieutenant Peatfield and 2nd Lieut. Thompson carried out the impedimenta, ladders and blankets, etc. to the head of the Sap at point of departure.

At 2.30 a.m. the men were lined up in the Sap.

At 2.45 a.m. the head of the party left the Sap and crawled out towards a point in the German line previously selected and noted by compass bearing, 150 degrees magnetic.

Although the moon was obscured by cloud, a Sniper fired upon the party on leaving the Sap and Bombs were thrown from the North but no damage was done. The head of the party reached the cover of thistles about 15 yards from the German wire and there awaited our Artillery fire.

The first salvo was fired at 3 a.m. whereupon the party rose up and walked to the wire.

The German wire was damaged but not wholly cut and the ground about the wire was cut up by shell holes.

The wire was 12 to 18 yards in depth and was successfully crossed by blanket bridges.

The bombing party entered the Trench and proceeded to block it in accordance with the previously arranged programme.

The centre party found a German Dug-out at point of entry. 2nd Lieut. Thompson threw a Bomb down the Dug-out, wounding some of the occupants, who were ordered in German to come out, with a threat that further Bombs would be thrown. They obeyed and prisoners were taken and escorted back to our lines.

The party was in the German Trenches about ten minutes.

The morale of the prisoners was exceedingly low, and they were so terrified that it was only with great difficulty they could be induced to come out of their Trench.

The party was recalled at point of entry by Code-word, and retired in good order, bringing one of our party, who was wounded and helpless.

Much time was lost in getting both German and our wounded out of the Trenches, and again crossing the wire with the casualties on the return journey. When the whole party had successfully evacuated the German Trench, I handed over command to 2nd.Lieut.Thompson as I felt weak from loss of blood, and feared I might have to be carried back.

In all four prisoners were taken, two of whom were, I think, wounded.

The Artillery Fire was accurate and effective.

A further report from 2nd Lieut. Thompson will follow.

During the raid 2nd Lieut. Thompson acted with the greatest coolness and courage. The success of the raid in a great measure is due to his work.

The conduct of the men left nothing to be desired.

The Germans manned a little Trench running South from point of entry immediately behind the main trench, and it was from this point that the Bombs were thrown.

I laid a paper chase trail when going out which was extremely useful on the return journey.

11/9/16.

STATEMENT BY 2/LIEUT. THOMPSON.

We went over and met with absolutely no opposition till we were in the German Trench, except from one Sniper.

We were absolutely unopposed going over, except for one man in the Trench, who they got out at once.

Corporal Jones' party ran on then and went up and blocked the Left Sap, but I stuck to the Dug-out just where we entered the Trench.

The next thing was I stood at the Dug-out door and ordered them to come out. I kept on shouting .... and I caught two of them coming out, whom I passed back to the man behind me, but whom it was I could not say, though I don't know about the dug-out on the Left.

The next thing was I sent to Mr. Peatfield if we should send the word "retire".

As I got the word passed along I went to the bottom of the steps where I met the fellows and got them to report when all were in. They climbed up the ladders and got out.

The last party to come out was Corporal Jones' party, and two of them got left.

Corporal Jones came running back to me to say he had a badly wounded man, and I immediately went back and we shouted to some of the men to help him up the ladder.

We stood and bombed the Trenches left and right while they were being got up. At any rate we got them up, and the man that was hit on the ladder. I got another man to help.

Both the covering party as well as the Bombers were got back.

Nobody else was hit and we got together a little covering party.

Corporal Jones, Sergeant Quinton and Corporal Blick stayed behind and it took them a considerable time to get them down to the sap. We held the Sap head until I got the word passed up that the final party had got into the Dug-out.

Then I called in the covering party and got them into the Paris Redoubt and got them all down into the Dug-out somehow, after which I crawled down myself. It was some time before I could make sure that everybody was in.

11/9/1916.

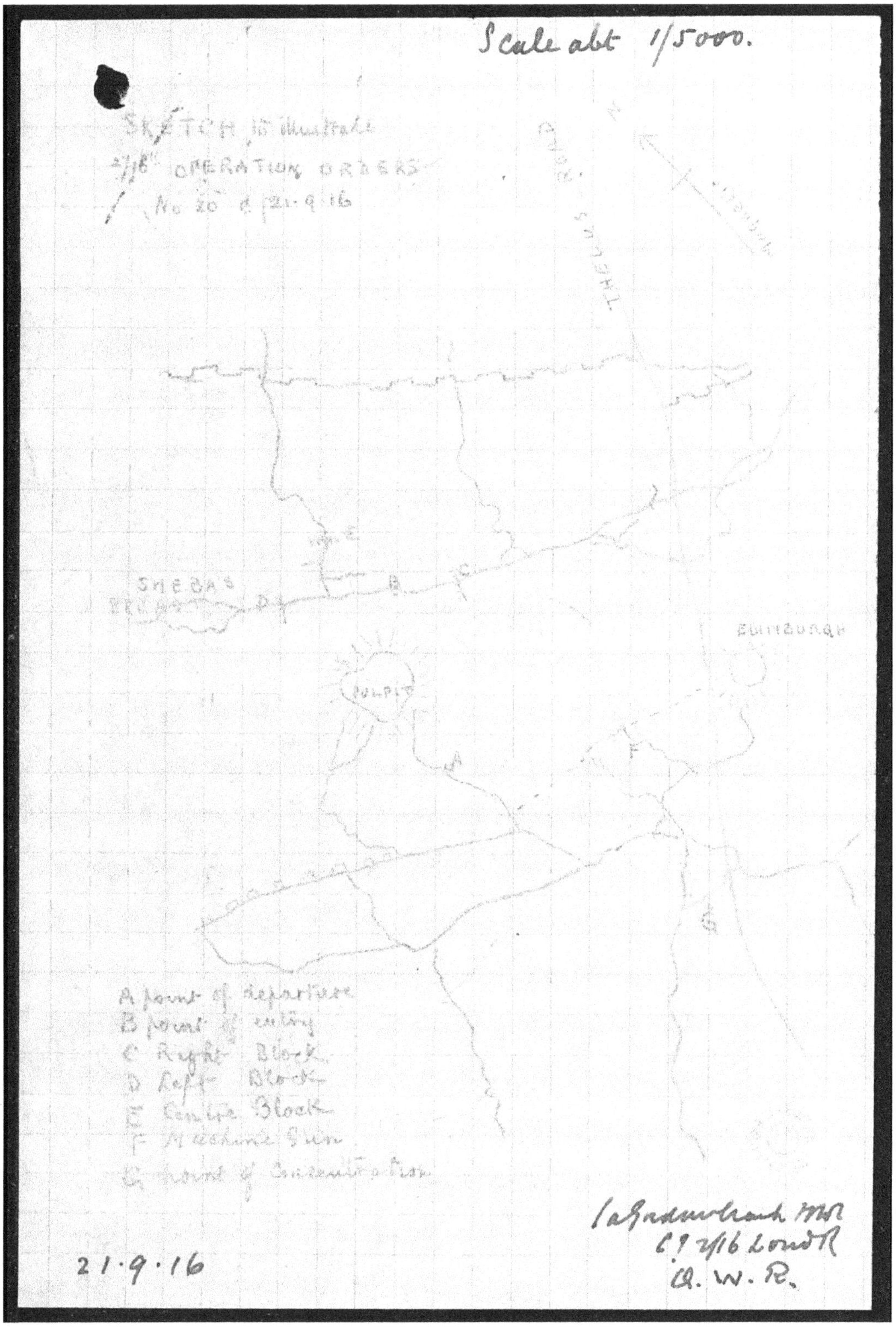

Scale abt 1/5000.
SKETCH to illustrate
2/16 OPERATION ORDERS
No 20 d/21·9·16
THELUS ROAD
SHEBAS BREAST
PULPIT
EDINBURGH
A
B
C
D
E
F
G
A point of departure
B point of entry
C Right Block
D Left Block
E Centre Block
F Machine Gun
G point of Concentration
21·9·16
2/16 Lond R
Q. W. R.

Appendix XIII

REPORT ON RAID CARRIED OUT IN ACCORDANCE WITH MY OPERATION ORDERS NO. 20 dated 21st SEPTEMBER 1916.

1. The Raid was successfully accomplished at 11 p.m. on 23/9/16. The Raiders left the PULPIT CRATER SAP at 10.55 and were all back in our Trenches by 11.30 with the exception of one wounded men.

2. Five prisoners were taken belonging to the 104th Regiment XIX Saxon Corps. 1 N.C.O. and 4 men; one of the latter being wounded in the head by a club. The number of German casualties in addition is estimated at from 14 to 20.

3. Our casualties were 2 men seriously wounded, 4 slightly wounded, 1 wounded and missing.

4. On starting the raiding party came under steady rifle fire from a covering party in front of Enemy wire, some 50 yards to our Right. This was the cause of most of the casualties. The Officer in Command however judging that this covering party would come under our barrage fire as soon as it started, waited for the signal and then held on for his objective.
The Trench was found to be full of Germans and contained several Dug-Outs.
The Trenches were of chalk, 8½ feet deep, very narrow with narrow fire step and in bad condition, only occasional pieces of revetment being seen. No duck-boards, traverses very broad, parados very high indeed.

5. The Enemy with one or two exceptions ran away rather than fight, certain men used their Rifles well but none accepted close fighting.

6. All the arrangements made were rigidly adhered to and answered their purpose well.

7. The Howitzer fire was most accurate, the Stokes Barrage was well carried out and was seen to cause a casualty to a Rifleman standing up on the parapet.
The 2" T.M. of y60 which had been asked to fire on a certain emplacement opposite LICHFIELD CRATER, silenced the Machine Gun with its first shot after it had fired 25 shots.
The Enemy's T.M.s replied and he also fired some half dozen 77 on our Support Line, presumably at the decoy lights.

8. The Medical arrangements worked well, from the Aid Post in firing Line to Advanced Dressing Station was a straight run.

9. After the Raid Officers Patrols went out and searched the whole of NO MAN'S LAND for a wide stretch for the man who fell wounded between the tapes on going out and must have crawled away before the return of the Raiding Party. Every yard was gone over under a continuous Rifle Fire and when near enough to hostile lines sharp bomb showers. Lights were also thrown along the ground which burst into two red balls.

10. The careful attention to all details given by Captain C.H. FLOWER contributed greatly to the success of the Raid.
The very skilful leading and resourceful bravery of LIEUT. S. HIPWELL was undoubtedly the cause of the success of the Raid. He was ably seconded by 2/Lieut. W. MORTIMER.
All the N.C.Os. and men behaved exceedingly well and in every case are reported to have carried out the duties allotted to each with accuracy and joyful alacrity.
I wish to collect further details of individual actions, and report further. Meanwhile I hope that Lieut. S. HIPWELL and 2/Lieut. W. MORTIMER may be considered for special mention.

P.T.O.

11. A further report will be prepared after receipt of written reports from the Officers engaged.

(sd) C.A.GORDON CLARK.
Lieut-Colonel,
Comdg. 2/16th LONDON REGIMENT.

24th September 1916.

SECRET. Copy Appendix XIV

REPORT ON RAID CARRIED OUT BY THE 2nd Bn. LONDON SCOTTISH ON THE GERMAN FRONT LINE IN ACCORDANCE WITH MY OPERATION ORDERS No.1.

Ref:- Accompanying Map.

1. The Raid was successful in that (i) Prisoners were captured.
(ii) Identifications obtained.
(iii) Casualties caused to enemy.

2. Information gained:-

(A) Enemy's Trenches. The Enemy's Trenches at A.16.a.98.98. to A.16.d.99.03. were in good repair and and about 8 feet deep. The parapet was built up with Sandbags, and the Fire Step was built up with ordinary brushwood + stake revetting. The trench had bays of about 30', these were not revetted. The trenches were wide - about 8' - at the top, and very narrow at the bottom, about 1'. They were very roughly made and had only one layer of sandbags on the top of the parapet and no sandbag revetting. The trenches were dry, but apparently not boarded.

There were no dug-outs.

(B) Enemy's wire. The wire on the front of this part of the trench is within 10 yards of the parapet. It consists for the most part of low coils of French Wire with Barbed Wire intertwined. The French Wire is pegged down. There was no trip wire at this point. This wire seems to be put up in a very unscientific manner.

The L.T.M. appears to have been very considerably more effective on the wire than the 2", which ranged short.

(C) No-Man's Land. There are a number of large shell holes just beyond the old French trench. There seemed to be no shell holes in the immediate vicinity of the German Front Line.

3. Prisoners taken:- (A) 1 Zug (Coy.Colour Sergt).
(B) 1 Corporal.
(C) 3 Private Soldiers.
Belonging to:- 107th Reserve Inf. Regt,
XVII Reserve Division,
XIV Saxon Corps.

4. All identifications and trophies were immediately forwarded to your H.Qrs.

5. Our casualties:- (A) Killed - 1 Corporal, 1 Private.
(B) Wounded - 1 Sergeant, 3 Privates.
(C) Missing - 1 Private.

6. Conduct of Officers:-

I wish to bring to your special notice Lieut. T.D.O.Maclagan. I cannot speak too highly of the trainer and leader of this Party. He worked out every detail in training, and by careful personal reconnaissance of the Ground was able to lead his Party confidently and successfully. He remained out till the last and helped with wounded. It is largely due to him that the enterprise proved so successful.

I would also like to bring to your special notice 2nd Lt. C. Tennant, who was in command of the Support Party. He rendered invaluable service. He had reconnoitred the

S E C R E T.

Sheet 2.

ground many times before. He noticed, and through his action promptly stopped, a counter-attack by the enemy from Point "L" on Map. By prompt action when the Artillery ceased fire he signalled to Batteries to open fire again and thus neutralised Enemy's rifle fire and enabled Raiding Party to retire with few casualties. He sent men out to help O.C. Raiding Party in with Corpl. Bantoft's body. He subsequently went out under my directions with Pte. Ross and searched No-man's Land for the missing private. He showed great presence of mind and coolness throughout.

2nd Lt. W.J.Bethume, though a young officer, proved most helpful and gallant. He is certainly worthy of consideration. He personally aided in capturing prisoners.

7. Conduct of Other Ranks:-

No.4780, Sgt. G.F.A.Jilbert behaved in a most gallant way. His Blocking Party met with considerable opposition. Though wounded in both thighs he continued to command his party and endeavoured to get Cpl. Bantoft back, the latter being mortally wounded.

No.4681, L/Cpl. R. Scott displayed great coolness and his conduct throughout was praiseworthy, and I wish specially to bring him to your notice.

I need not add the whole ~~Rxxkx~~ of the Raiding Party and Support Party behaved in a soldierlike manner and worthy of the regiment they represented.

8. Stokes Gun:- I would like to point out the good services rendered by O.C. L.T.M's, 179th Bde. These guns' barrage on either flank clearly marked the boundary of Attack. Their fire was rapid and effective.

9. Artillery. The Barrage put up by the Artillery was most effective and well placed, and the points specially chosen as Targets seemed to entirely keep down Machine Gun fire.

10. M.T.M. The O.C. 2" Guns, 179th Bde. was active on the ARGYLL GROUP. The O.C. 2" Guns, 181st Bde. Co-operated in this action.

11. M.Gs. The O.C. 179th Machine Gun Company aided on Raiding Party's Left Flank during the early part of Raid.

12. Lewis Guns. The Lewis Guns of the Battalion fired on ARGYLL ~~xxxxx~~ CRATER and one gun accompanied Support Party under 2nd Lt. C. Tennant, though, owing to its advanced position, did not come into action.

13. Rifle Grenades. Rifle Grenades were used as a feint by O.C. "A" Coy. also a Searchlight and lamp. Aerial Torpedoes were fired ~~at them~~.

14. Whistles. Whistles were used by O.C. "A" Coy. but proved useless.

S E C R E T.

Sheet 3.

15. Medical Arrangements. The R.M.O's arrangements were well carried out, but the Advanced Dressing Station were collecting and evacuating wounded from the Aid Post in the Elbe. was slow –

16. Methods Adopted. The Methods adopted for these operations I have requested the leader of the party to specially comment on these and make any suggestion he thinks advisable.

17. Further Reports. Any subsequent information will be forwarded for your information.

18. Officers' Statements. I attach the 3 Officers' statements.

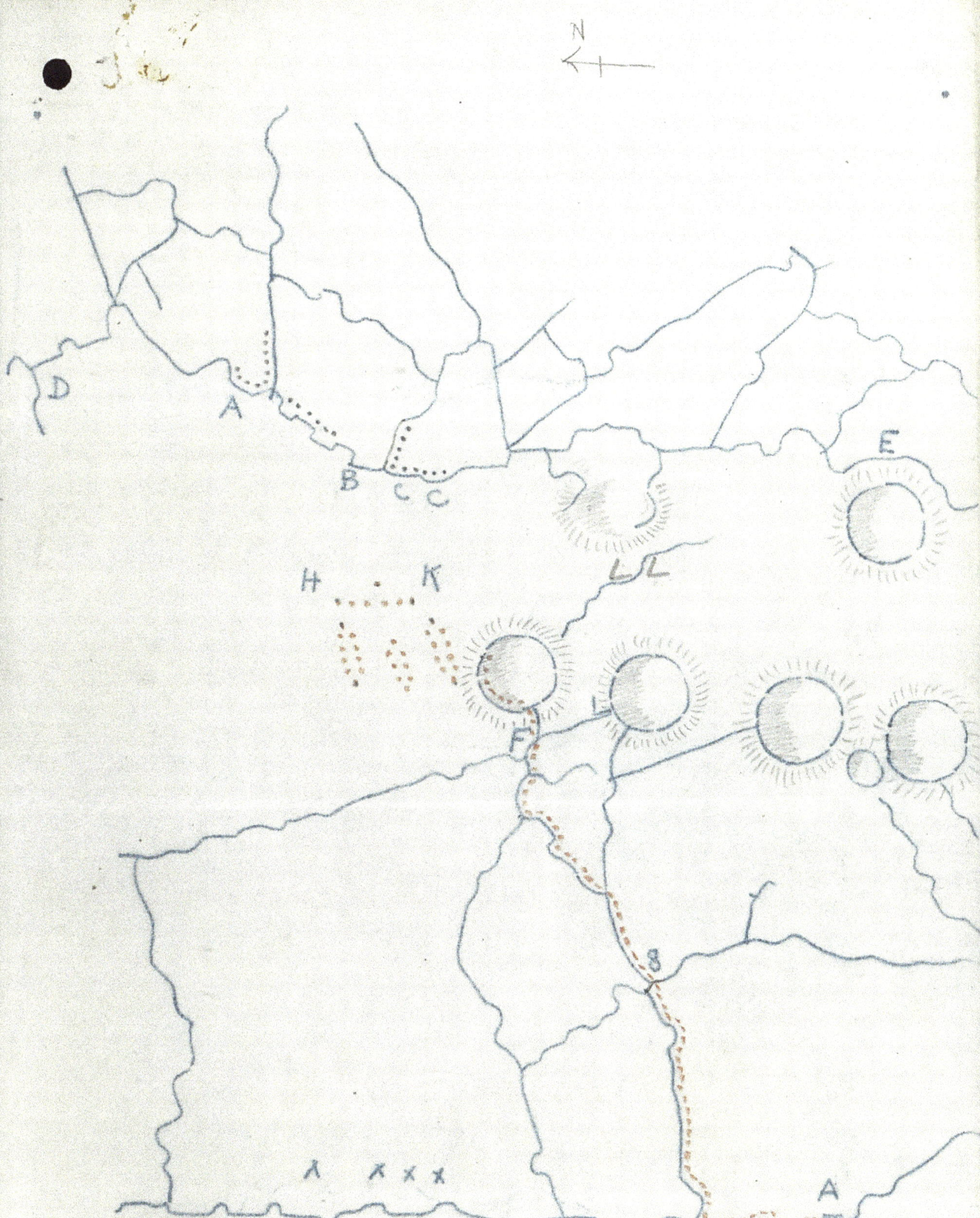
N
D
A
B
C C
H
K
LL
E
F
S
A
J

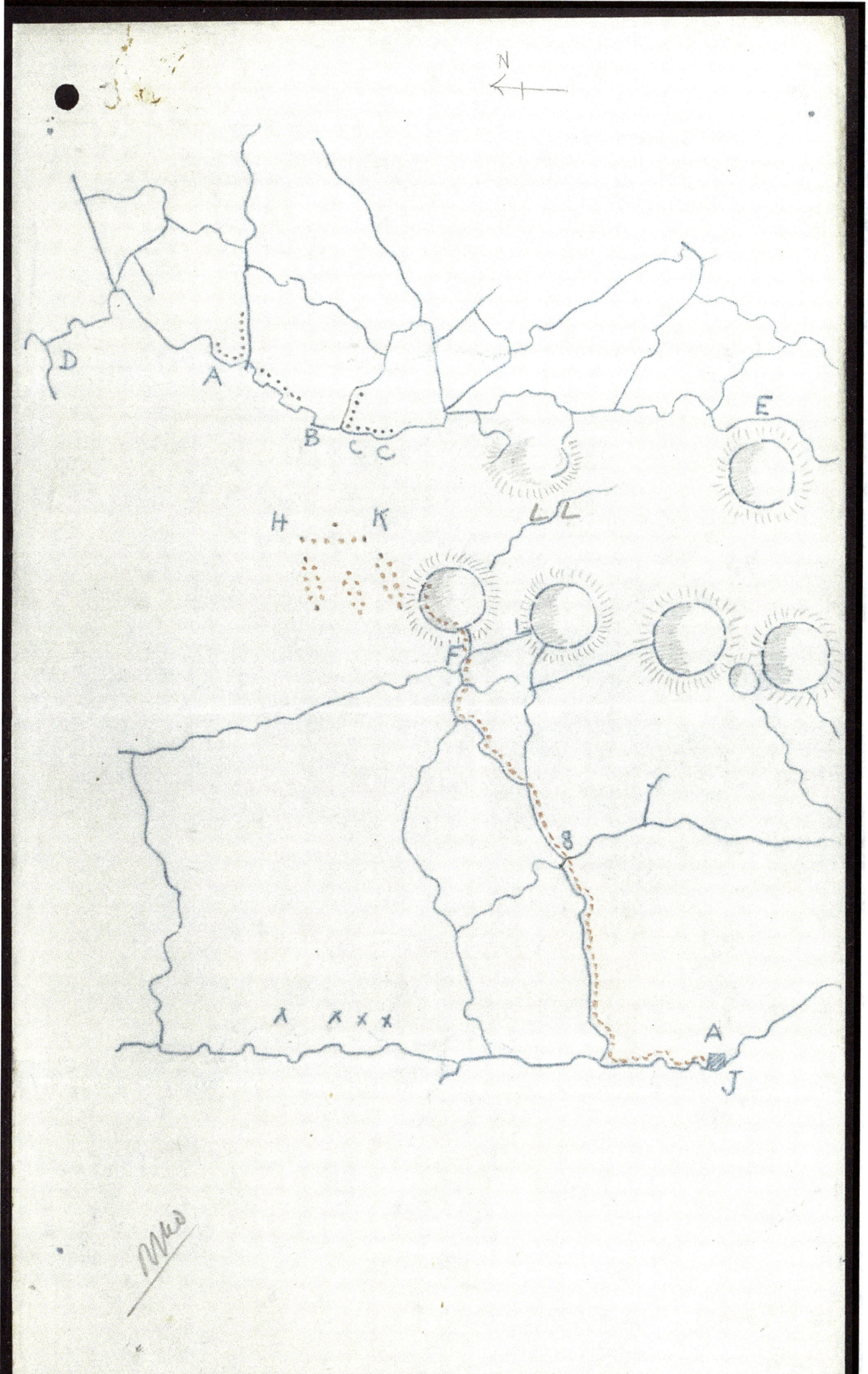

Report of Support Party. 30 - 9- 16.

Positions occupied as ordered overlooking Craters and Enemy Saps. (2 minutes before Zero.)
Sent message per 'Phone to continue barrage after 2.31.am. to protect wounded men and portion of party in "No Man's Land".
Enemy observed leaving Sap (left) dispersed by our rifle fire only. (2.35.am.)
Cpl.Cumming and Pte.Mee (C.Coy.) particularly distinguished themselves in bringing back wounded Men into Sap, and later in Search Party for missing men, working throughout the night. Withdrew Support Party when ordered by Lt.Maclagan.

- - - - - - - - - - -

Report Clearing Party. 30 - 9 - 16.

All Equipment and arms cleared from French trench this morning, 7.15.am. On return from Search Party.
Barbed wire replaced in BORDES Sap, and telephone wiring taken away.

- - - - - - - - - -

Search Party Report.

4.15.am. - 5.am.

Made examination of ground in front of old French Firing line, and around left Crater.
No success.

6.am. - 7.45.am.

Inspected ground in the vicinity of early morning action.
Could find no trace whatever.
Ground very difficult - long grass - and shell holes - Snipers very active this morning.
Search to be continued.

- - - - - - - - - -

O Tennant (2nd Lt)

Report on Raid carried out by 1/14th Bn. London Regt.
(London Scottish) on the night 29th/30th
September, 1916.

The C.O., Filby.

I have the honour to report in connection with the above that my party assembled at the rendezvous at midnight on the night in question, and after preliminary inspections, etc. we proceeded up BORDER SAP, past Crater marked "F" on plan, crawled into the old French Trench out of which the wire had previously been removed and the barricade thinned down. Compass bearings were then taken at a point about 30 yards along the trench and our objective - the extreme left of a prominent clump of brushwood - established during previous reconnaissances, was identified. My party then proceeded towards this objective and at three minutes before Zero I and my scouts were at a point about 30 yards East of the old French Trench. Here I arranged my parties in proper formation and all ranks were warned of the proximity of Zero. The night was very dark, further bearings were taken here and the line of advance confirmed. At Zero the party went forward at a bound. We were detected by the Germans, who fired on us. On reaching the wire I found it uncut, but about 10 yards to my left I recognised a high tangle of French wire, to the left of which I knew a gap had been cut by our T.M's on the previous day. I immediately directed my Left Blocking Party (Sgt. Jilbert), and Body Snatching Party (Lieut. Bethune), to rush a party of about eight of the enemy in the fire trench. This was most successfully executed by both parties. Two at least of this party of Germans were killed, the Sergeant, Corporal and three men being taken prisoners. The covering party meanwhile took up its station on the parapet and the ladders were placed in the Trench. The Right Blocking Party also took up its position and got into the Enemy's Trench without opposition. Great difficulty was experienced in getting the prisoners out of the trench. When this was done the code word for withdrawal was passed down to both Blocking Parties. The Right Blocking Party withdrew without difficulty but the Left Blocking Party had sustained 2 casualties; and Sgt. Jilbert, who, although wounded in both legs, and could only crawl with difficulty, still kept his party under perfect control. We experienced great difficulty in getting the other wounded man (Cpl. Bantoft) out of the trench. The Artillery barrage ceased as we were getting this wounded man clear of the wire. The enemy then opened a heavy fire on us. We retaliated, firing into their trenches with our revolvers.

2nd Lt. Tennant, immediately grasping the situation, telephoned for further Artillery support, which was prompt in reply. He also sent up two men to our assistance and thus enabled me to get Corpl. Bantoft back. He died before reaching our lines. On reaching the Support Party I ordered Mr. Tennant to withdraw.

On reaching the dug-out (rendezvous) I at once called the roll and found that two men of the Body Snatching Party could not be found. They were not seen by any of their party to enter the German Trench. Search was subsequently made for them by 2nd Lt. Tennant and Pte. Ross, but no trace of them could be found.

In connection with the night's work the following arrangements made for the conduct of the raid were of great value to us.

(1) The three minutes' allowance given before Zero.

Sheet 2.

This enabled me to get control of my party before moving forward.

(2) The final formation adopted in No-man's Land enabled me to keep control and get my parties into the German Trench. This formation also proved of special value owing to the darkness of the night. It enabled us to get into the trench together, saved casualties, and accelerated operations.

(3) The first salvo for the Artillery to start was extremely beneficial.

(4) The pause at the end of 10 minutes gave us warning of the time and helped to control operations.

(5) The Advanced Signalling Station enabled the Officer responsible to cover our retirement, getting the Artillery to re-open when he found that the party had not returned to time.

(6) Compass bearings were of the greatest assistance. The night being very dark the Very lights sent up on the flank helped us to recognise previously selected landmarks in No-man's land.

I should like to bring under notice the extremely gallant behaviour of Sgt. Jilbert, L/Cpl. R. Scott and Pte. Ross. Sgt. Jilbert, although wounded in both legs, kept control of his party and assisted us to lift out of the trench and bring back under fire the wounded N.C.O. of his party (Cpl. Bentoft). L/Cpl. Scott carried Cpl. Bentoft on his back part of the way across No-man's Land under fire until a ladder ~~was obtained~~ and further help were obtained. After that he carried Sgt. Jilbert for some distance, who meanwhile had become greatly exhausted. The behaviour ~~throughout~~ of both those N.C.Os. throughout the night was magnificent. Pte. Ross also helped to carry back Cpl. Bentoft under fire and went out subsequently with Mr. Tennant to search for the missing men of the Body Snatching Party.

J. D. O. Maclagan Lt.

30/9/1916.

B.O. Filly.

APPENDIX.

The positions of the Germans found in the part of German Trench which we found was as in the following sketch :-

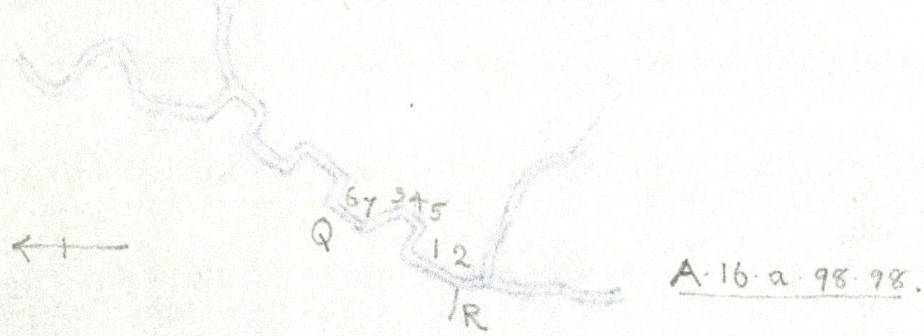

The Left Blocking Party got into the trench at Q. and worked to its left and captured Nos. 6 & 7.

Germans Nos. 4 & 5. were killed in the trench. They were evidently killed by our rifle fire as we entered the trench. No. 3. was the sergeant taken after some resistance.

Nos. 1 & 2. were the private and corporal captured at the post marked R. which we found.

(SD) Wm. J. BETHUNE.

COPY.

Sir,

I have the honour to report that I led the body snatching party into the German Trenches after the Right Blocking Party. All my party with the exception of the two men who are missing jumped into the trench and were fired on from inside the trench and immediately we became engaged with a German N.C.O. who put up a strong resistance. After trouble with him for three minutes we managed to get him over the parapet and handed to our covering party. We next came across a sentry post where we found the youngest prisoner who was very willing to give himself up. He held up his hands and called out several times, "Mercy, Scottish". He was got over the parapet at once and handed to the covering party. A third prisoner was found immediately in the trench, he spoke English and started to offer resistance but was soon overpowered and handed out of the trench. At this point + 11 I gave the order to withdraw and we got out of the trench and ordered the party to get back by the tape. I awaited till I saw the right blocking party clear and then thinking that all was right on the ~~tege~~ left - the left blocking party was not within my vision - I retired in my turn. The Artillery stopped when I reached BORDES sap.

With regards to the two missing men, they were not seen by anyone in the German trench, entering it or even in "No Man's Land".

I also beg to report that the men of my party worked splendidly, although they had strong opposition and were underfire.

I have the honour to be, Sir,
Your obedient servant,

(SD) Wm. J. BETHUNE. 2nd. Lieut.

APPENDIX.

APPENDIX XV

179th Infantry Brigade.

CASUALTIES FOR THE MONTH OF SEPTEMBER 1916.

UNIT.	KILLED.	WOUNDED.	MISSING.	TOTAL.
2/13th Battalion London Regiment	2.	23.	-	25.
2/14th Battalion London Regiment	9.	*57.	2.	68.
2/15th Battalion London Regiment	6.	19.	-	25.
2/16th Battalion London Regiment	6.	47.	1.	54.
179th Machine Gun Co.	-	1.	-	1.
179th Light Trench Mortar Battery	-	2.	-	2.
60x Medium Trench Mortar Battery	-	-	-	-
	23.	149.	3.	175.

*Includes 2 accidental. N.B. This does not include the Officers' casualties shewn below:-

OFFICERS WOUNDED:-

2/14th Battalion London Regiment:- Lieut. T. G. O. COGGIN.

2/15th Battalion London Regiment:- Captain K. W. M. PICKTHORN. (Accidental)

Lieut. B. PEATFIELD. (M.C.)

2/Lieut. G. E. THOMPSON. (D.S.O.)

APPENDIX XVI

179th Infantry Brigade.

STRENGTH RETURN.

As at SEPTEMBER 1ST. 1916.

UNIT.	OFFICERS.	OTHER RANKS.
179th Infantry Brigade Headquarters	12.	52.
2/13th Battalion London Regiment.	29.	919.
2/14th Battalion London Regiment	40.	939.
2/15th Battalion London Regiment	41.	926.
2/16th Battalion London Regiment	35.	988.
179th Machine Gun Co.	10.	144.
179th Light Trench Mortar Battery	4.	46.
60x Medium Trench Mortar Battery	2.	23.
	173.	4037.

This Return includes Officers, N.C.Os. and Other Ranks attached from other Units.

179th Infantry Brigade.

STRENGTH RETURN.

As at 30th SEPTEMBER, 1916.

UNIT.	OFFICERS.	OTHER RANKS.
179th Infantry Brigade Headquarters	9.	51.
2/13th Battalion London Regiment:	41.	913.
2/14th Battalion London Regiment:	40.	968.
2/15th Battalion London Regiment:	44.	973.
2/16th Battalion London Regiment:	46.	969.
179th Machine Gun Co.	10.	161.
179th Trench Mortar Battery:	4.	46.
	194.	4081.

This Return includes Officers, N.C.Os. and Other Ranks attached from Other Units.

APPENDIX XVII

CONFIDENTIAL.

179th Infantry Brigade. W.I.R.8.

WEEKLY INTELLIGENCE SUMMARY.

For Week ending September 5th 1916.

GENERAL SUMMARY. Artillery has not been consistently active during the past week, intermittent firing relieved by occasional bombardments at particular points occurring at intervals.

SHEBAS BREASTS received considerable attention but little real damage appears to have been done, except to the trenches immediately behind, which must have severely suffered. The enemy have a wholesome dread of our T.M. fire both 2" and 3", as whenever we open they immediately cease firing.

Our M.G's have carried out indirect fire schemes nightly.

Our L.G's have been moderately active on enemy front line parapets and NO MANS LAND. Owing to the number of our wiring parties and patrols, great care has had to be exercised with the firing of this weapon.

The relief of the 2/15th and 2/16th by the 2/13th and 2/14th Battalions London Regiments was completed on the night of 31/8/16 and 1/9/16.

Enemy artillery has on the whole been feeble, although certain points of our front and support lines have suffered considerable damage notably OLD & NEW DOUBLEMONT, PARIS RED. and LICHFIELD & STOKE ST's.

Whizz bangs, rifle grenades, and small salvos of aerial torpedoes have been favourite forms of hostile annoyance. The search light S.E. of THELUS has been observed on 2 occasions.

An enemy relief is suspected to have taken place on the night of 3/4/9/16 opposite our right sub sector.

Considerable enemy activity has been noticed in ARGYLL GROUP of CRATERS.

Aerial activity in the early portion of the period under review was considerable, the weather of the last few days hasinterfered and has also made observation very difficult.

The wiring along our front has been considerably strengthened and improved. Patrols have been out nightly reporting little enemy activity in this direction.

The following positions have been located during the past week.

T.M's at A 16 a 95.80.
" " A 4 d 60.89
" " A 4 d 28.67.
" " A 10 b 45.63.
" " A 10 b 50 .92.
O.P. at A 16 a 99.58.
" " A 16 a 95.45.
M.G. " A 16 b 00.40. & A 16 b 05.07.
Snipers post A 16 c 85.75.
SNIPERS BAGS 3 hits claimed.

SEPTEMBER 6th 1916.

BRIGADIER GENERAL
179th Infantry Brigade.

CONFIDENTIAL. W.I.R. 9.

179th Infantry Brigade.

WEEKLY INTELLIGENCE SUMMARY.

For Week ending September 12th 1916.

GENERAL SUMMARY.

During the period under review the Enemy blew a Mine forming the CLAUDOT GROUP of CRATERS, there now being three CRATERS adjoining. Verification of this by aerial photography would be of advantage. The work of consolidation is now practically completed. A new Observation Line running from MERFILLAT to the OLD CLAUDOT has been constructed as well as a good O.P. in the Northern LIP of the NEW CRATER.

A camouflet was blown by the Enemy in front of BORDES SAP but without breaking ground.

The Mine blown on the 7th instant PHILLIP GROUP has not been consolidated and the Enemy have made no attempt on their side.

A successful raid on hostile Trenches took place in the early morning of the 11th resulting in the capture of 4 live prisoners, our casualties being slight.

Various white flags are distributed over Enemy Sector opposite this Front.

Enemy Artillery has been distinctly more active on the whole, ~~of~~ the ELBE and our Support Line generally receiving considerable attention from 77's, 5.9's and 4.2's.

Our Stokes Gun in the vicinity of STAFFORD ST. is evidently causing the Enemy particular annoyance as he has spent much Ammunition in searching for it.

Hostile Patrols have been more active on several occasions approaching our SAPS, but ~~on~~ every ~~occasion~~ time were easily dispersed.

The general attitude of the Enemy seems apprehensive, the wild Rifle Firing at night, his increased patrolling of NO MAN'S LAND, coupled with the Artillery registering previously reported, points to this.

Wiring along our Front has been considerably strengthened and improved. Aerial activity has been considerable, our planes appearing to fly recently at lower altitudes when patrolling.

The weather on the whole has not been good for observing and the bright moonlight has interfered with Patrol work.

The following have been located:-

OBSERVATION POSTS	at	A.16.c.70.92.
	and	A.16.a.96.69.
T. M's	at	A.4.b.60.07,
	and	A.4.b.65.06, (alternative position).

SNIPERS' BAG:- 5 hits claimed.

Bde. H.Q.
September 13th 1916.

BRIGADIER GENERAL,
Comdg 179th Infantry Brigade.

CONFIDENTIAL. W.I.R. 10.

179th Infantry Brigade.

WEEKLY INTELLIGENCE SUMMARY.

For Week Ending September 19th 1916.

GENERAL SUMMARY.

The past week may be summarised as quiet on the whole, nothing of particular or outstanding importance having characterised the period under review.

Our Artillery, T.M's and L.T.M's have been moderately active bombarding special points on Enemy Front and Support Lines and cutting hostile wiring which at night has been kept from repair. The enemy opposite our Left Front has been less active than the Troops opposed to our Right Sub-Sector.

OILCANS made their reappearance being fired from a point opposite BENTATA SAP (38A) and from the back of ARGYLE GROUP of CRATERS. An Enemy Relief is suspected to have taken place on the night of 17/18th.

Patrols have been out nightly examining both our own and hostile wiring, Enemy activity in this direction very slight.

Aerial activity on our part has been considerable, whereas only 2 Enemy Machines have been seen and they patrolled well within their own Lines. On 3 occasions balloons were up behind and N. of THELUS.

Wiring along our Front has been steadily strengthened, and increased.

The weather generally has been bad for observation, and particularly in the early part of the week, the Moon interfered with reconnaissance in NO MAN'S LAND.

The following have been located:-

T.M. at A.16.a.98.55.
" A.16.c.70.50.
" A.4.d.44.99 (strongly suspected).

SNIPERS' POST: A.16.c.74.92.

SNIPERS' BAG: Hits claimed: 5.

Bde. H.Q.
September 20th 1916.

BRIGADIER GENERAL,
Comdg 179th Infantry Brigade.

CONFIDENTIAL. W.I.R.11.

179th Infantry Brigade.

WEEKLY INTELLIGENCE SUMMARY.

For Week Ending September 26th 1916.

GENERAL SUMMARY.

All operations during the past week may be stated, without undue optimism, to have been successful, and have certainly been the means of instilling increased confidence into the troops holding this Sector Front.

Enemy reply to our Artillery has been weak, his T.M. fire decidedly less and beyond spasmodic bursts directed on favourite and particular Targets such as MOWCOP, MILL and ZIVY on our Left, and PARIS, BENTATA and SUPPORT Lines on our Right Sub-Sectors, his activity has been principally confined to desultory aerial torpedo fire not many of his new Mortar Shell; considerable anti-aircraft and M. G. (at night) fire.

The most important operation during the period under review was the successful raid by a party of the 2/16th Battalion London Regiment on the night of the 23rd instant, five prisoners being taken. Enemy wire has been methodically cut and kept open.

The ARGYLE CRATER GROUP has been (to mention only one of many targets) well bombarded and the contours on enemy side altered to the great advantage of our observation, and as our T.M's, both 2" and 3" have been extremely active, firing at least 3 shots to one, the nervous attitude shewn by the increase in flares sent up, the aimless bombing of, and the absence of Patrols in NO MAN'S LAND, is very apparent. Our Patrols have been out nightly.

Our M.G's have carried out nightly Brigade programmes, and our Lewis Guns have assisted in preventing hostile wire repairing, and in dispersing Working Parties.

Aerial reconnaissance owing to the recent improved weather conditions has been daringly and actively conducted. One of our planes was brought down on our own Territory on the 25th instant, and one yesterday morning appeared to be somewhat crippled, as when last seen flying towards ECOIVRES it appeared to be swaying about considerably. Wiring work has continued on both our Sub-Sectors, that on the right being rather more interfered with by hostile M.G. fire than on the Left Sub-Sector.

Trench repair work owing to the heavy rain of last week has been arduous.

The following have been located:-

T.M. at A.4.d.64.86.
" " A.4.d.07.90.
" " A.4.d.26.64.
" " A.4.d.42.53.
(suspected) A.16.c.74.65.
SNIPERS POSTS) at A.10.b.35.97.
or O.P's.) A.16.a.98.32.
~~A.16.a.73.15.~~
A.16.c.95.60.
(Under construction) A.16.a.74.04.
(suspected) A.16.a.88.15.

SNIPERS' BAG: Hits claimed: 6.

Bde. H.Q.
September 27th 1916.

BRIGADIER GENERAL,
Comdg. 179th Infantry Brigade.

Secret

Vol 5

179th Infantry Brigade Headquarters

War Diary

Volume 5

October 1916

31. 10. 16.

Instructions regarding War Diaries and Intelligence Summaries are contained in F. S. Regs., Part II. and the Staff Manual respectively. Title Pages will be prepared in manuscript.

WAR DIARY 179 Inf. Bde

or

~~INTELLIGENCE SUMMARY~~

(Erase heading not required.) OCTOBER 1916 VOLUME. 5.

Army Form C. 2118.

Place	Date	Hour	Summary of Events and Information	Remarks and references to Appendices
TRENCHES NEUVILLE St VAAST	Oct 1.		Quiet day nothing to record	
	2.		Some activity on part of Enemy T.M.s which did great damage to parts of trenches but caused few casualties	
	3.		A wet day clearing up in the evening when Enemy Shelled BENTATA using aeroplane observation.	
	4		G.O.C. proceeded to Rear Headquarters en route for England on leave A quiet day	
	5th		Lt. Col. C. Gordon Clark assumed command of 179th Bde. in absence of Brig. Genl. Baird on leave. Major W. N. Herbert. Bde Major 179th Bde proceeded to take command of 1st Batt. Northumberland Fus. Capt. G. W. Sherston assumed duties of Bde. Major 179th Inf. Bde.	[illegible]
	6th		Enemy T.M's exceptionally active - causing considerable damage to ARGYLE ST. knocking in one dugout and blocking ARGYLESAP. ~~[illegible]~~.	[illegible]

1875 Wt. W593/826 1,000,000 4/15 J.B.C. & A. A.D.S.S./Forms/C. 2118.

Instructions regarding War Diaries and Intelligence Summaries are contained in F. S. Regs., Part II. and the Staff Manual respectively. Title Pages will be prepared in manuscript.

WAR DIARY
or
~~INTELLIGENCE SUMMARY~~

(Erase heading not required.)

Army Form C. 2118

Place	Date	Hour	Summary of Events and Information	Remarks and references to Appendices
Trenches NEUVILLE ST. VAAST.	Oct. 7th		Usual Trench Mortar activity. TERRITORIAL. C.T. damaged in afternoon by heavy enemy Trench Mortar. Our Light Trench Mortars damaged some new enemy earthworks and silenced a light enemy T.M.	
	8th		Our Stokes Trench Mortars damaged enemy front line trenches between ARGYLE and PARIS Group of Craters. Enemy's T.M. and Artillery continued more active - considerable damage being done in vicinity of ARGYLE, the MILL, and ZIVY. Battn on our Right raided enemy trenches on our immediate right capturing four prisoners, Bde. on our left carried out raid capturing six prisoners.	
	9th		Enemy T.M's again active - causing more damage to ARGYLE St.	
	10th		Nothing to record.	
	11th		Enemy attempted a raid on our front line - 2.A.M. he put up a barrage of T.M's for an hour - everything was then quiet till 5am when he repeated his barrage with Field guns - 4.5 Hows & T.M. - This barrage lasted till 6.10 am, during which time ~~the~~ two parties of approximately 15 men each attempted to enter our lines by Sap. 60.A. in vicinity of PULPIT Crater - They found our posts very much on the alert, and never succeeded in getting beyond our saps - Our posts accounted for 8 Germans Killed 1 wounded + 1 unwounded prisoner belonging to 133rd Regt. Our casualties were all caused by the enemy barrage.	

1875 Wt. W593/826 1,000,000 4/15 J.B.C. & A. A.D.S.S./Forms/C. 2118.

Instructions regarding War Diaries and Intelligence Summaries are contained in F. S. Regs., Part II. and the Staff Manual respectively. Title Pages will be prepared in manuscript.

WAR DIARY
or
~~INTELLIGENCE SUMMARY~~ 98

(Erase heading not required.)

Army Form C. 2118

Place	Date	Hour	Summary of Events and Information	Remarks and references to Appendices
Trenches NEUVILLE ST. VAAST	Octr 12th		Enemy Trench Mortars less active ~~with~~ excepting in vicinity of the PULPIT which was intermittently bombarded all day and badly damaged. The dead body of a German was brought in from SAP 61.A. This man belonged to 12th Pioneers.	9S
	13th		Inter-Battalion relief took place in early morning without casualties. Intermittent enemy Trench Mortaring all day. replied to by our Stokes and 2".	9S
	14th		Our Stokes very active. considerable damage being done to enemy front line wire.	9S
	15th		Nothing to record. G.O.C. returned to Rear Headquarters from leave.	9S
	16th		An organized bombardment on enemy Trench Mortars positions and enemy Trenches took place. Artillery of all calibres from 12" to 18 pr. took part in this bombardment. also our 9.45 Trench Mortar fired for the first time on this sector. considerable damage appeared to be done to the enemy trenches. but Enemy Trench Mortars were not silenced	9S

1875 Wt. W593/826 1,000,000 4/15 J.B.C. & A. A.D.S.S./Forms/C. 2118.

Army Form C. 2118

WAR DIARY
or
~~INTELLIGENCE SUMMARY~~

(Erase heading not required.)

Instructions regarding War Diaries and Intelligence Summaries are contained in F. S. Regs., Part II. and the Staff Manual respectively. Title Pages will be prepared in manuscript.

Place	Date	Hour	Summary of Events and Information	Remarks and references to Appendices
Trenches NEUVILLE ST VAAST.	Oct 16th		as they bombarded our trenches again at night and carried out an organised bombardment on our right and left sectors the next day. The firing of our 9.45 T.M. was somewhat erratic. a few shells falling very short. The body of a dead german was brought in at night from Stafford Crater.	EL
	17th		Enemy bombarded our Trenches heavily with T.M's. Causing considerable damage.	EL
	18th		Enemy again bombarded our Trenches with T.M. more damage. G.O.C. & Bde. Major went down to Rear Headquarters for Corps Commanders inspection of 2/14th Battn. G.O.C. inspected all 1st Line Transport. Returned to Advanced Headquarters in evening.	EL
	19th		Inter-Battalion reliefs took place without casualties. Enemy Trench Mortars did considerable damage to Left Sub-Sector. Our Artillery and T.M's were active during the day	EL

Instructions regarding War Diaries and Intelligence Summaries are contained in F. S. Regs., Part II. and the Staff Manual respectively. Title Pages will be prepared in manuscript.

WAR DIARY
or
~~INTELLIGENCE SUMMARY~~ 9l

(Erase heading not required.)

Army Form C. 2118

Place	Date	Hour	Summary of Events and Information	Remarks and references to Appendices
			contd.	
TRENCHES NEUVILLE ST. VAAST.	19th		doing considerable damage to enemy front line.	
	20th		Enemy T.M's again active but suppressed by our Artillery.	9l
	21st		An enemy aeroplane was brought down by Lewis gun fire.	9l
	22nd		Nothing unusual to record. Advanced parties of 9th Canadian Infantry Brigade came to visit our lines prior to taking over. C.O's & Adjts. of Battalions. Intelligence Staff Capt. & Signalling Officer	9l
	23rd		Company commanders of incoming Battns of 9th Canadian Infantry Brigade came up to go round the line. A quiet day with nothing to report.	9l 17th Bde. Op. Order No. 19. for Relief of 17th Bde by 9th Can. Inf. Bde. attached.

1875 Wt. W593/826 1,000,000 4/15 J.B.C. & A. A.D.S.S./Forms/C. 2118.

Army Form C. 2118

Instructions regarding War Diaries and Intelligence Summaries are contained in F. S. Regs., Part II. and the Staff Manual respectively. Title Pages will be prepared in manuscript.

WAR DIARY
or
~~INTELLIGENCE SUMMARY~~ 9/
(Erase heading not required.)

Place	Date	Hour	Summary of Events and Information	Remarks and references to Appendices
TRENCHES NEUVILLE ST VAAST	Oct 24th		Br. Genl. Hill commanding 9th Can. Inf. Bde came up to advanced Headquarters and stay the night. inspecting the line during the day.	
			A very quiet day - absence of enemy T.M. activity particularly marked - 2/13 Battn in Left Subsector and 2/16 in Bde.	9/
	~~25th~~ 9/		Reserve relieved by 43rd and 60th Battn Can. Inf. respectively.	
			Relief effected with no casualties. 179th M.G. Coy, 179th T.M.B relieved by 9th Can. M.G. Coy & C/9 T.M.B. respectively. No casualties.	
			2/15 marched from TILLOY-HERMAVILLE to SERICOURT.	
	25th		Major STEINER Bde. Major 9th Can. Inf. Bde came up and was taken round front line by Bde. Maj. 179 Bde.	
			2/14 relieved by 52nd Battn Can. Inf. relief completed without casualties.	9/
			2/16 relieved by 58th Battn Can. Inf. in Div. Res. in BRAY.	
			179th Bde. Hd. Qrs went down to ÉCOIVRES for the night.	
			2/13 march from BOIS des ALLEUX to SAVY	
ÉCOIVRES	26th		Bde. Hd. Qrs marched to BUNEVILLE & billeted	
			2/14 marched to TILLOY-HERMAVILLE from MAROEUIL	9/
			2/16 " " SIBIVILLE " TILLOY-HERMAVILLE	
			179th M.G. Coy " " BUNEVILLE " " "	
			179th T.M.B " " " " ÉCOIVRES.	

Instructions regarding War Diaries and Intelligence Summaries are contained in F. S. Regs., Part II. and the Staff Manual respectively. Title Pages will be prepared in manuscript.

WAR DIARY
or
~~INTELLIGENCE SUMMARY~~
(Erase heading not required.)

Army Form C. 2118.

Place	Date	Hour	Summary of Events and Information	Remarks and references to Appendices
BUNEVILLE	Oct. 27th		2/13 marched from SAVY to BUNEVILLE & billeted	
			2/14 " " TILLOY & HERMAVILLE to MONTS-en-TERNOIS	
			1st Army Commander met Brigadiers of 60th Divn at Divl. Hd. Qrs. Conference at Divl. Hd. Qrs.	
			Brigadier & Bde. Maj. visited 2/15 & 2/16 Battns in morning.	
	28th		Bde. marched South to WAVANS area.	
			Units billeted for night as follows:-	
			2/13 - NOEUX / BOFFLES	
			2/14 - FORTEL.	
			2/4 Fd. Ambce / 2/15 - BEAUVOIR.	
			2/16 - VILLERS l'HOSPITAL.	
			Bde. Hd. Qrs. / M.G. Coy / T.M.B. / 2/4 Fd. Coy RE - WAVANS.	op. or No. 20 & Amendment attached

1875 Wt. W593/826 1,000,000 4/15 J.B.C. & A. A.D.S.S./Forms/C. 2118.

Army Form C. 2118

Instructions regarding War Diaries and Intelligence Summaries are contained in F. S. Regs., Part II. and the Staff Manual respectively. Title Pages will be prepared in manuscript.

WAR DIARY
or
~~INTELLIGENCE~~ SUMMARY 21

(Erase heading not required.)

Place	Date	Hour	Summary of Events and Information	Remarks and references to Appendices
	Oct 29th		The Brigade marched South from WAVANS area to RIBEAUCOURT area. A very wet day and roads very heavy. Units were billeted as follows:- Bde. Hd. Qrs. } M. G. Coy. } T. M. By. } RIBEAUCOURT. 2/13 ---- PROUVILLE 2/14 ---- MONTIGNY les JONGLEURS. 2/15 ---- { LANCHES (H^d Q^rs) { BARLETTE { ST. HILAIRE. 2/4. Fd. Coy. RE. } 2/4. Fd. Amce } PROUVILLE. Orders received in evening for 2/4 Fd. Coy. to proceed soon as possible to TOUTENCOURT for work under C.E. Reserve Army.	
RIBEAUCOURT	30th		Personnel 2/4 Fd. Coy. RE proceeded by lorry & Transport by road to TOUTENCOURT. Battns. commenced training. The day was spent	

1375 Wt. W593/826 1,000,000 4/15 J.B.C. & A. A.D.S.S./Forms/C. 2118.

Instructions regarding War Diaries and Intelligence Summaries are contained in F. S. Regs., Part II. and the Staff Manual respectively. Title Pages will be prepared in manuscript.

WAR DIARY
or
~~INTELLIGENCE SUMMARY~~

(Erase heading not required.)

Army Form C. 2118.

Place	Date	Hour	Summary of Events and Information	Remarks and references to Appendices
ALBERTVOURT	Oct. 30th		doing Physical Training - Close order drill - etc - Conference of Commanding Officers at Bde. Hd. Qrs in afternoon.	
	31st		G.O.C. visited battalions to see 'Attack Drill' being practised. 2/13. 2/14 in morning. 2/15. 2/16 in afternoon. A very wet day.	

LIST of APPENDICES.

XVIII.	179th Inf. Bde. Op. Order No. 19. dated 20th October 1916
XIX.	" " " " " No. 20 dated 25th " 1916
XX	" " " " " No. 21. dated 27th " 1916
XXI	" " " " " No. 22. dated 28th " 1916
XXII	Weekly Intelligence Summaries.
XXIII	Strength states for 1st + 31st of month.
XXIV	Casualties for month of October.

E Sherston Capt
Bde. Major. 179 Inf Bde

1375 Wt. W593/826 1,000,000 4/15 J.B.C. & A. A.D.S.S./Forms/C. 2118.

Appendix - XXII

CONFIDENTIAL. W.I.R.12.

179th Infantry Brigade.

WEEKLY INTELLIGENCE SUMMARY.

For week ending October 3rd 1916.

GENERAL SUMMARY.

Our Artillery has fired intermittently throughout the week. On the 2nd instant our 4.5 HOWS damaged O.P's at A.16.c.72.70 and A.16.a.97.35.

Our M.T.M's have been active on wire cutting at various points, and L.T.M's in addition to dispersing numerous Working Parties have consistently harassed Enemy from repairing his wiring as well as cutting in several places. M.G's have carried out nightly indirect Fire Schemes and L.G's have fired on gaps in wiring and on hostile Working Parties.

Enemy artillery has been very inactive, whereas his T.M. fire in particular has steadily increased, doing a considerable amount of damage, especially with the heavy T.M. to our Trenches generally. Particular objectives have been nearly the same as last week, with the exception that STAFFORD ST. and STONE ST. have replaced MOWCOP and ZIVY to a great extent on the Left Sub-Sector Area. Hardly any difference has been observed in the number of Aerial Torpedoes, Sling Bombs, and Rifle Grenades sent over. A spirit of nervousness still exists, shewn by the throwing of Bombs into his own wire, and a continuance of the wild Rifle Fire previously reported. The number of VERY Lights sent up has on the average been lower.

Hostile aerial activity has increased.

A successful raid was carried out by the 2/14th Battalion London Regiment under Lieut. MacLagan on the night of 30th September 1916 resulting in the capture of 3 prisoners, one being a Sergt.Major. Very careful observation and bearings taken during the past few days have located TWO of the Heavy T.M's as firing from each end of the New Trench running from A.11.a.10.03 to A.11.a.05.30.(SANDER GRABEN to an off shoot of the KEMPEER WEG). The Shells from these T.M's are about 27" long by 6" in dia. and make a hole some 15' in dia. The explosion is very violent.

The weather has not been favourable for observing.

WINTER has replaced SUMMER time since October 1st.

Patrols have been out nightly but no Enemy activity in this direction has been encountered.

Trench repair and wiring work has been considerable. Enemy Working Parties have been heard, but little result noticed.

The following have been located:-

T.M. Emplacement at	A.16.b.30.50.
" " "	A.16.b.95.40.
" " "	A.10.d.30.30.
" " "	A.11.a.10.03.
" " "	A.11.a.05.30.
M.G. Emplacement at	A.10.b.36.74.
" " "	A.10.b.35.12.
" " "	A.16.a.93.62.

SNIPERS claim 3 hits.

Bde. H.Q.
October 4th 1916.

BRIGADIER GENERAL,
Comdg 179th Infantry Brigade.

CONFIDENTIAL. W.I.R.13.

179th Infantry Brigade.

WEEKLY INTELLIGENCE SUMMARY.

For week ending October 10th 1916.

GENERAL SUMMARY.

The past week has seen a notable increase in hostile T.M. activity, and greater damage has been done to this Sector Front than during any period since we took over. The main objectives on the Left Sub-Sector have been the MILL Area, PHILLIP and LOSANGE SAPS, FIRING LINE from about Centre, Northwards to PULPIT, the PULPIT CRATER and SAPS, MERCIER and TERRITORIAL about its Junction with FIRING LINE. On the Right Sub-Sector PARIS REDOUBT and ARGYLE ST. and BAIRD ST. and vicinity have suffered greatly.

Coloured lights have increased in numbers and appear to be used as directing lines for T.M. fire. A pigeon was observed flying from the direction of THELUS due E. over our Lines about 3.30 p.m. on 3rd October 1916. Hostile aeroplanes have been rather more active, flying over our Lines on two occasions.

Noise of blasting has been reported as follows:-

near PULPIT CRATER 7 & 9.5 a.m. on 3/10/16.
8 a.m. & 6.45 p.m. on 5/10/16.
near LONG SAP 11.30 p.m. on 9/10/16.

A new type of Sling Bomb is now in use by the Enemy having a delayed fuse action.

Hostile Sniping at night has largely decreased. The customary M.G. fire on our Front Line Parapets continues throughout the night.

The work in conjunction with repairing Trenches caused by Enemy T.M. fire has been very arduous. Patrols have been out nightly. Considerable wiring has been carried out.

The following have been located:-

T.M. Emplacement	at	A.16.d.55.25.
" "	"	A.16.b.68.50.
" "	"	A.4.d.58.90.
Sentry Post	"	A.4.d.37.16.
" "	"	A.4.d.43.60.
Snipers' Posts	"	A.10.b.35.80.
" "	"	A.10.b.42.76.

SNIPERS claim 3 hits.

Bde.H.Q.
October 11th 1916.

LIEUT-COLONEL,
Comdg 179th Infantry Brigade.

CONFIDENTIAL.

179th Infantry Brigade. W.I.R.14.

WEEKLY INTELLIGENCE SUMMARY.

For week ending October 17th 1916.

GENERAL SUMMARY:

Hostile T. Mortaring has if anything increased in intensity this past week, and very considerable damage throughout the Sector Front has been caused. The Enemy raided our lines near the PULPIT CRATER on the morning of the 11th but were driven off, leaving one dead, one wounded, and one unwounded prisoner in our hands besides suffering considerable casualties whilst returning to his own lines, as also subsequently when searching for missing raiders in NO MAN'S LAND on the following night.

An Artillery straffe of considerable magnitude on hostile T.M. Emplacements, Front and Support Lines generally took place on the 17th instant. Our Stokes Guns have been active throughout the week keeping Enemy wire open and dispersing Working Parties,

M.G's have carried out nightly indirect fire schemes and L.G's have done good work in firing at and dispersing Working Parties.

Aerial activity has been considerable throughout the week.

The weather on the whole has not been good for observation.

Patrols have been out nightly.

Wiring has been somewhat hindered by the Moon as also by the call for repairs to Trenches, the work entailed being extremely arduous.

The LETTER BOX opposite VICTOIRE (A.16.c.70.72) despite some 9 reported direct hits, is still in position.

The following have been located:-

L.T.M. at A.10.b.30.80.
T.M. at A.16.d.55.25.
T.M. at A.16.b.68.50.
T.M.(Suspected) at A.16.b.40.80.
T.M.(Suspected) at A.10.b.50.18.
Oilcans at A.10.d.13.13.
Small Aerial Torpedoes at A.16.b.04.35 & A.16.a.99.80.
M.G. at A.16.a.98.86. (suspected).
M.G. at A.10.d.00.22.
Snipers Post at A.16.a.90.37.
DUMP (suspected) at A.17.a.18.60.

SNIPERS claim 6 hits.

Bde.H.Q.
October 18th 1916.

BRIGADIER GENERAL,
Comdg. 179th Infantry Brigade.

CONFIDENTIAL. W.I.R.15.

179th Infantry Brigade.

WEEKLY INTELLIGENCE SUMMARY.

For Week Ending October 24th 1916.

GENERAL SUMMARY:

The past week has seen a continuance of hostile T.M. activity, and very considerable damage to Trenches and Dug-outs has resulted, as well as knocking out a 3" Gun and completely destroying one of our Machine Guns.

The work involved in getting and keeping Trenches cleared has been exceptionally arduous.

Aeroplane activity has been considerable, more so on the Enemy's part than previously noticed here, very accurate smoke bomb direction of fire being observed. Hostile activity on the part of Snipers and Patrols in NO MAN'S LAND at night has during the past week been NIL.

Weather on the whole has not been good for observation.

The following have been located:-

LOOPHOLE PLATES at A.10.b.35.86.
O.P. at A.10.b.47.63.
OILCAN position at A.10.d.13.13.
LETTER Box, still in position, at A.16.c.70.72.
DUMP increased in size at A.17.a.18.60.
T.M's suspected at A.4.b.69.05 and A.10.b.80.05.
M.G.Emplacement at A.4.d.40.32 (SHEBAS BREASTS).

SNIPERS claim 2 hits.

Bde.H.Q.
October 25th 1916.

BRIGADIER GENERAL,
Comdg 179th Infantry Brigade.

APPENDIX. XVIII

SECRET. 179th Infantry Brigade. Copy No. 16

OPERATION ORDERS. Friday, 20th October 1916.
NO.19.

1. The 179th Infantry Brigade will be relieved by the 9th Canadian Infantry Brigade - during the period 23rd - 25th October 1916.

2. Reliefs will be carried out in accordance with attached March Table.
Battalion Commanders will hand over command of their Sectors on completion of Relief.
Completion of relief of each Unit to be reported to Brigade Headquarters by the code word "JOY".

3. 179th Machine Gun Co. will be relieved by Machine Gun Coy., 9th Canadian Infantry Brigade on the 23rd and 24th instants - half the Company on each day -.
Details of Relief to be arranged between O's C. Machine Gun Companies concerned.
Relief to take place after dark each day.

4. 179th Stokes Mortar Battery will be relieved by Stokes Mortar Battery on the 24th instant. Details of relief to be arranged between O's C. Batteries concerned.

5. Guides consisting of 1 Officer and 8 N.C.O's per Battalion, 1 Officer and 2 N.C.O's per Trench Mortar Battery, 1 Officer of Machine Gun Coy. and 1 man per Vickers Gun in the Line will be detailed in accordance with Appendix "A" to guide incoming Units into the Line.
These guides are to remain with the Unit they guide into the Trenches until the 27th instant. They will report to REAR BRIGADE HEADQUARTERS in ECOIVRES at 10 a.m. on that day.
In addition to the above, Brigade Signal Section will leave 3 linesmen behind, who will also report at Rear Headquarters at 10 a.m. on the 27th instant and be conveyed to New Area by lorry.
All the above will be rationed and quartered by the Unit to which they are attached, but they are to have rations with them for the day following the first day of their attachment.

6. All Maps up to the scale of and including 1/20,000 are to be handed over to relieving Units, receipts being obtained. All Maps 1/40,000 and upwards will be retained.

7. Receipts are to be obtained for all Trench Stores handed over. These receipts are to be forwarded to Brigade Headquarters by 6 p.m. on the 28th instant. Instructions as to exactly what is to be handed over in the way of Trench Stores will be issued later.

8. Advanced Parties will come to this Area on the 22nd and 23rd instant. Details of these Parties and instructions regarding them are shown in Appendix "B" attached.

9. These orders only take Units as far as the present Back Area. Further Orders will be issued regarding the move from Back Area to New Area.

10. Refilling Points will be notified later.

11. Billeting Parties will report as laid down in Appendix "C"

12. Acknowledge.

Captain,
BRIGADE MAJOR,
179th Infantry Brigade.

Copy No. 1: Retained.
2: Staff Captain.
3: 9th Canadian Infantry Brigade.
4: 2/13th Battalion L.R.
5: 2/14th Battalion L.R.
6: 2/15th Battalion L.R.
7: 2/16th Battalion L.R.
8: 179th Machine Gun Co.
9: 179th Trench Mortar Battery.
10: 2/4th Field Co. R.E.
11: 180th Infantry Brigade.
12: 181st Infantry Brigade.
13: 60th Division.
14: Brigade Transport Officer.
15: Brigade Signalling Officer.
16: War Diary.

No.	Date.	UNIT.	FROM.	TO	Time of March.	Relieving Unit.	Time Relieving Unit leaves Back Area.	Route for Incoming Unit.	Route for Outgoing Unit.	REMARKS.
1.	Oct.23.	2/15 Battn. L.R.	BRAY.	TILLOY & HERMAVILLE.	As relieved.	43rd Battn. Canadian Infantry.	-	-	(HAUTE-AVESNES (TILLOY - (HERMAVILLE.	MARCH: By Coys.at 200 yards Interval.
2.	Oct.24.	2/13 Battn. L.R.	TRENCHES C.3. Left Sub-Sector.	BOIS de ALLEUX MONT ST. ELOY. ECOIVRES.	As relieved.	43rd Battn. Canadian Infantry.	BRAY 5 p.m.	BRAY-Main HOUDAIN-ARRAS Rd. BRUNEHAUT Farm - AUX RIETZ. GUILLERMOT TRENCH.	TERRITORIAL AUX RIETZ - by Road to BRUNEHAUT Farm - Main ARRAS - HOUDAIN Rd.	By Platoons at 100 yards Interval.
3.	Oct.24.	2/16 Battn. L.R.	BRIGADE RESERVE.	BRAY.	As Relieved.	60th Battn. Canadian Infantry.	MAROEUIL 2 Right Coys. 8 p.m. 2 Left Coys. 8.30 p.m.	2 Left Cos BRUNEHAUT FARM - AUX RIETZ GUILLERMOT TRENCH. 2 Right Co. SAPPER TRENCH - DOUAI.	2 Left Coys. TERRITORIAL TRENCH - AUX RIETZ BRUNEHAUT FARM. 2 Right Cos. CLAUDOT TRENCH to ARRAS - BETHUNE RD.	By Platoons at 100 yards Interval.
4.	Oct.24.	179th T.M. Batty.	TRENCHES.	ECOIVRES.	As Relieved.	T.M.B. 9th Canadian Infantry Brigade.	To be arranged between O.C's concerned.	To be arranged between O.C's concerned.	To be arranged between O.C's concerned.	-
5.	Oct.25.	2/14 Battn. L.R.	TRENCHES. C.1. Right Sub-Sector.	MAROEUIL.	As Relieved.	52nd Battn. Canadian Infantry ~~Brigade.~~	MAROEUIL. 5.30 p.m.	MAROEUIL SAPPER TR. FRONT LINE.	TERRITORIAL TR. AUX RIETZ BRUNEHAUT FARM - MAROEUIL.	By Platoons at 100 yd Interval.
6.	Oct.25.	Bde.H.Q.	A.8.d.25.	ECOIVRES.	On completion of Relief.	9th Canadian Inf. Brigade.				

APPENDIX "A".

Guides as mentioned in Para. 5 of Brigade Operation Order No. 19 will report as follows:-

Battalion.	Personnel.	Report to.	At.
2/13th.	1 Officer. 8 N.C.O's.	Headquarters, 43rd Battalion Canadian Infantry, BRAY.	2 p.m. on the 24th instant.
2/14th.	1 Officer. 8 N.C.O's.	Headquarters, 52nd Battalion Canadian Infantry, MAROEUIL.	3 p.m. on the 25th instant.
2/16th.	1 Officer. 8 N.C.Os.	Headquarters, 60th Battalion Canadian Infantry, MAROEUIL.	4 p.m. on the 24th instant.

Bde.M.G.Co. 1 Officer for Headquarters and at least 1 N.C.O. per Section to be arranged between C.O's concerned.

T.M.By. To be arranged between C.O's concerned.

Units are to ensure that the above Guides know all the Routes which they are to guide incoming Units along. They should also know all there is to know about the portion of the Front Line which they are to show to Incoming Units.

APPENDIX "B".

ADVANCED PARTIES.

1. Advanced Parties will visit this Area on the 22nd and 23rd instants.

2. These parties will consist on the 22nd instant of:-
(a) 3 Commanding Officers, who will each visit his opposite number in the Line.

1 Representative of each of the following:-
Brigade Machine Gun Co.
3" Stokes Trench Mortar Battery.
Field Co., R.E.
Intelligence Staff Captain.

(b) 1 Representative per Battalion)
1 Representative Brigade Headquarters) to

remain at REAR and get information as regards Transport Lines, Q.M. Stores, etc.

On the 23rd instant every Company Commander who is coming into the Line will come up.

The arrangements for the above parties are as follows:-

They will arrive at REAR BRIGADE HEADQUARTERS, ECOIVRES at 10 a.m. on each day by bus where they will be met by a Guide from Brigade Headquarters, who will bring them to Advanced Brigade Headquarters.

On the 22nd instant O.C. Units are to arrange to have a Guide at Advanced Brigade Headquarters at 12 noon to guide their opposite numbers to their Headquarters.

On the 23rd instant each Battalion is to send a runner to Advanced Brigade Headquarters to guide the Company Commanders of the incoming Battalion, up to Brigade Headquarters, where the C.O. will see that they are passed on to Company Commanders concerned.

All the above will return to their Units the same night.

APPENDIX "C".

BILLETING PARTIES.

Oct. 23rd. 2/15th Battalion will send billeting party to report to TOWN MAJOR, HERMAVILLE, at 10 a.m.

Oct. 24th. 2/13th Battalion will send billeting party to report at Rear Brigade Headquarters, ECOIVRES, at 2 p.m.

2/16th Battalion will send billeting party to report at Rear Brigade Headquarters, ECOIVRES, at 2 p.m.

3" Stokes Mortar Battery will send billeting party to report at Rear Brigade Headquarters at 2 p.m.

Oct. 25th. 2/14th Battalion will send billeting party to report to TOWN MAJOR, MAROEUIL, at 2 p.m.

Oct. 23/24th. Brigade Machine Gun Co. will make its own arrangements for billets in ~~Rear~~ Back Area.

T123/20.
22/10/16.

SECRET.

179th Infantry Brigade.

1. Reference 179th Brigade Operation Orders No. 19 dated 20th October 1916, Units will march to the New Area in accordance with attached March Table.

2. The whole of the First Line Transport of each Battalion will March with the Battalion to the New Area.

3. Machine Gun Company will march to the new Area with the 2/16th Battalion L.R. O.C., 2/16th Battalion will issue orders for the march of this Unit.

4. Billeting Parties will go on at least four hours ahead of Units and will meet the Staff Captain or his Representative at the MAIRIE in each place to have billets allotted.

5. Instruction as regards Refilling Points, Supplies, etc. will be issued by Staff Captain.

6. Brigade Headquarters will be at A.8.d.5.2. till 6 p.m. on the 25th, when they will open at Rear Headquarters, ECOIVRES. They will close at ECOIVRES at 11 a.m. on the 26th, at which hour they will open at SERICOURT.

7. Acknowledge.

(sd) E. SHERSTON.
Captain,
BRIGADE MAJOR,
179th Infantry Brigade.

October 22nd 1916.

MARCH TABLE.

No.	UNIT.	DATE.	FROM.	TO.	Time at which Unit is to arrive at its destination.	ROUTE.	REMARKS.
1.	2/15th.	23rd.	BRAY.	TILLOY-HERMAVILLE.	As relieved.	HAUTE-AVESNES-HERMAVILLE-TILLOY.	Battalions may march in their own time but must arrive at their destination not later than the time stated in Col. 6.
2.	"	24th.	TILLOY-HERMAVILLE.	SERICOURT.	3 p.m.	HERMAVILLE-IZEL-LES-HAMEAU. VILLERS-SIRE-SIMON AMBRINES-and on via MAGNICOURT & HOUVIN.	
3.	2/16th. Machine Gun Co.	25th.	BRAY.	TILLOY-HERMAVILLE.	As relieved.	Same as No. 1.	
4.	"	26th.	TILLOY-HERMAVILLE.	2/16th:SIBIVILLE. M.G.Co: SERICOURT.	3 p.m.	Same as No. 2.	
5.	2/13th.	26th.	BOIS-DES-ALLEUX.	SAVY.	3 p.m.	ACQ-CAPELLE-FERMONT-AUBIGNY-SAVY.	
6.	"	27th.	SAVY.	BUNEVILLE.	3 p.m.	TILLOY-LES-HERMAVILLE. IZEL-LES-HAMEAU-VILLERS-SIRE-SIMON-AMBRINES-MAGNICOURT-HOUVIN-BUNEVILLE.	The Band will play battns. into billets in New Area from 2 miles outside the village they are going to.
7.	2/14th.	26th.	MAROEUIL.	TILLOY-HERMAVILLE.	3 p.m.	Same as No. 1.	
8.	"	27th.	TILLOY-HERMAVILLE.	MONTS-EN-TERNOIS.	3 p.m.	Same as No. 2 as far as HOUVIN. then direct to destination.	
9.	Bde.H.Q.) 179th T.M.B.)	25th.	ECOIVRES.	SERICOURT.	-	Same as No. 2.	
10.	2/4th Fld. Co.R.E.	25th.	FERME DOFFINE.	BUNEVILLE.	3 p.m.	VILLERS-SIRE-SIMON AMBRINES MAGNICOURT-HOUVIN-BUNEVILLE.	

2/4th Field Ambulance will be billeted in MONTS-EN-TERNOIS but will march under orders to be issued by A.D.M.S. 60th Division.

No. 2 Coy. A.S.C. will be billeted in MONCHEAUX and will march under orders to be issued by O.C. Divisional Train.

AMENDMENT TO 179TH BRIGADE T.123/20 dated 23/10/16.

UNITS WILL BE BILLETED AS FOLLOWS:-

Brigade Headquarters. 179th Machine Gun Co. 179th Light Trench Mortar Battery. 2/4th Field Co. R.E. 2/13th Battalion.	BUNEVILLE.
2/14th Battalion. 2/4th Field Ambulance.	MONTS-EN-TERNOIS.
2/15th Battalion.	SERICOURT and HONVAL.
2/16th Battalion.	SIBIVILLE.
No. 2 Coy.A.S.C.	MONCHEAUX.

Captain,
BRIGADE MAJOR,
179th Infantry Brigade.

Bde.H.Q.
October 24th 1916.

APPENDIX. XIV

SECRET:

Copy No. 12

179th Infantry Brigade.

OPERATION ORDERS NO. 20.

WEDNESDAY, October 25th 1916.

Reference Map:
LENS Sheet 11
1/100,000.

1. 179th Brigade will march South from the NEW AREA on the 28th October 1916.

2. Units will march in accordance with attached March Table.

3. Billeting Parties will report to Staff Captain at the CHURCH in VACQUERIE-LE-BOUCQ at 10 a.m. on the 28th October 1916.

4. First Line Transport complete, will march in rear of each Battalion.

5. Refilling Point will be on DOULLENS-AUXI-LE-CHATEAU Road between FROHEN-LE-GRAND and Road Junction about 2 miles W. of that place. Time will be notified later.

6. Divisional Headquarters will be at FROHEN-LE-GRAND. Brigade Headquarters will be at WAVANS.

7. The Village in which each Unit will be billeted will be notified later.

8. Attention is directed to the last sub-para. of Para. 7, Divisional Standing Orders. The Report mentioned must be rendered as soon as possible after arrival.

9. Reports during the March to Head of Column. After arrival in Billets to Brigade Headquarters, WAVANS.

10. Acknowledge.

G Sherston

Captain,
BRIGADE MAJOR,
179th Infantry Brigade.

October 25th 1916.

Copy No. 1: Retained.
2: 2/13th Bn.
3: 2/14th Bn.
4: 2/15th Bn.
5: 2/16th Bn.
6: 179th Machine Gun Co.
7: Light Trench Mortar Battery.
8: 2/4th Field Co., R.E.
9: 2/4th Field Ambulance.
10: No.2 Co., A.S.C.
11: 60th Division.
12: War Diary.

STARTING POINT

ROAD JUNCTION by S. of ST.HILAIRE.

....

ROUTE

FREVENT - VACQUERIE LE BOUCQ.

....

No.	UNIT.	Time head of each Unit passes Starting Point: Road Junc. by S. of St. Hilaire.	Route to Starting Point.
1.	Brigade H.Q. T.M. Battery. M.G. Coy. 2/4	10. a.m.	BUNEVILLE SIBIVILLE. SERICOURT.
2.	2/15th Bn.L.R.	10.4 a.m.	DIRECT.
3.	2/16th Bn.L.R.	10.14 a.m.	SERICOURT.
4.	2/13th Bn.L.R.	10.24 a.m.	Same as 1.
5.	2/14th Bn.L.R.	10.34 a.m.	MONCHEAUX SIBIVILLE SERICOURT.
6.	2/4th Fd.Co.R.E.	10.40 a.m.	Same as 1.
7.	2/4th Fd.Ambce.	10.45 a.m.	Same as 5.
8.	No.2 Coy.Divl.Train.	10.50 a.m.	SIBIVILLE SERICOURT.

APPENDIX. XX

Copy No. 12

179th Infantry Brigade.

OPERATION ORDERS, NO. 21.

....

FRIDAY, OCTOBER 27th. 1916.

Reference Operation Orders No. 20 dated 25th October 1916.

Units will be billeted as follows:-

1.	Brigade Headquarters. Light Trench Mortar Battery. 179th Machine Gun Co. 2/4th Field Co., R.E.	WAVANS.
2.	2/15th Bn.L.R.	BEAUVOIR. BEALCOURT.
3.	2/16th Bn.L.R.	VILLERS, l'Hopital.
4.	2/13th Bn.L.R.	BOFFLES & NOEUX.
5.	2/14th Bn.L.R. ..) .. .. 2/4th Field Ambulance)	FORTEL.

ROUTE:-

The Brigade will march along the following Route:- FREVENT - MAIN AUXI-LE-CHATEAU Road - through VACQUERIE-LE-BOUCQ - Cross Roads, ½ mile W. of M in MAMUR - NOEUX - WAVANS - BEAUVOIR - Riviere - BEALCOURT.

The Brigade will march intact as far as VACQUERIE-LE-BOUCQ.

Units will leave the Column at the following points and march to their Areas as under:-

UNIT.	LEAVE COLUMN AT.	DESTINATION.	ROUTE.
2/16th Bn.L.R.	VACQUERIE-LE-BOUCQ.	VILLERS l'Hopital.	via FORTEL.
2/13th Bn.L.R.	-do-	NOEUX & BOFFLES.	-do-
2/14th Bn.L.R.	-do-	FORTEL.	Direct.
2/4th Fld.Ambce.	-do-	FORTEL	Direct.

Previous Orders regarding Billeting Parties are cancelled. They will report according to instructions issued by Staff Captain under this Office No. S/Q/57(1) dated 26th October 1916.

[signature]

Captain,
BRIGADE MAJOR,
179th Infantry Brigade.

Copy No. 1: Retained.
2: 2/13th Bn.L.R.
3: 2/14th Bn.L.R.
4: 2/15th Bn.L.R.
5: 2/16th Bn.L.R.
6: 179th Machine Gun Co.
7: 179th L.T.M.Battery.
8: 2/4th Fld.Ambce.

Copy No. 9: 2/4th Fld.Co.R.E.
10: 60th Division.
11: Signalling Officer.
12: War Diary.

APPENDIX XXI

SECRET. Copy No. 12

179th Infantry Brigade.

OPERATION ORDERS NO. 22.

SATURDAY, OCTOBER 28TH. 1916.

1. 179th Brigade will march South from its present Area on the 29th October 1916.

2. Units will march in accordance with attached March Table.

3. Billeting Officers are going on in advance this evening, 28th. Billeting Parties will report to their respective Billeting Officers 3 hours in advance of their Units, as follows:-

   2/13th Bn.L.R.)
   Field Co.R.E.) CHURCH IN
   Field Ambulance.) PROUVILLE.
   No. 2 Coy.A.S.C.)

   2/14th Bn.L.R. MONTIGNY CHURCH.

   2/15th Bn.L.R.)
   2/16th Bn.L.R.) RIBEAUCOURT.
   179th Machine Gun Co.)

4. First Line Transport complete will march in rear of Units.

5. Refilling Point will be on ROAD between BERNAVILLE and FIENVILLERS.

6. Divisional Headquarters will be at BERNAVILLE.
   Brigade Headquarters will be at RIBEAUCOURT.

7. Reports during march to Head of Column. After arrival in Billets to Brigade Headquarters, RIBEAUCOURT.

8. Acknowledge.

Captain,
BRIGADE MAJOR,
179th Infantry Brigade.

Copy No. 1: Retained.
2: 2/13th Bn.L.R.
3: 2/14th Bn.L.R.
4: 2/15th Bn.L.R.
5: 2/16th Bn.L.R.
6: 179th Machine Gun Co.
7: 179th Light Trench Mortar Battery.
8: 2/4th Field Coy.R.E.
9: 2/4th Field Ambulance.
10: No. 2 Coy.A.S.C.
11: 60th Division.
12. War Diary.

STARTING POINT:

ROAD JUNCTION IN ST.ACHEUL.

No.	UNIT.	FROM.	TO	Time Head of Unit passes Starting Point.	ROUTE.
1.	Bde.H.Q. T.M.Battery. Machine Gun Coy.	WAVANS.	RIBEAUCOURT.	9.30 a.m.	BEAUVOIR. BEALCOURT. ST.ACHEUL. MONTIGNY. PROUVILLE. RIBEAUCOURT.
2.	2/15th L.R.	BEAUVOIR BEALCOURT	BARLETTE. EPECAMPS. ST.HILAIRE.	9.36 a.m.	ST.ACHEUL. MONTIGNY. PROUVILLE. RIBEAUCOURT.
3.	2/16th L.R.	VILLERS L'HOSPITAL	RIBEAUCOURT & DOMESMONT.	9.44 a.m.	WAVANS. then same as No.1.
4.	2/13th L.R.	NOEUX & BOFFLES.	PROUVILLE.	9.52a.m.	WAVANS, then same as No.1.
5.	2/14th L.R.	FORTEL.	MONTIGNY.	10.0 a.m.	VILLERS L'HOSPITAL WAVANS, then same as No.1.
6.	2/4th R.E.	WAVANS.	GRIMONT.	10.20 a.m.	Same as No.1.
7.	2/4th Fld. Ambce.	FORTEL.	PROUVILLE.	10.25 a.m.	Same as No.5.

179th Infantry Brigade.

STRENGTH RETURN.

As at 31st October, 1916.

UNIT.	OFFICERS.	OTHER RANKS.
179th Infantry Brigade Headquarters	9.	51.
2/13th Battalion London Regiment	43.	980.
2/14th Battalion London Regiment	41.	930.
2/15th Battalion London Regiment	46.	1,012.
2/16th Battalion London Regiment	46.	985.
179th Machine Gun Co.	8.	178.
179th Light Trench Mortar Battery.	4.	44.
	197.	4,180.

This Return includes Officers, and Other Ranks attached from other Units.

Appendix XXIV

179th Infantry Brigade.

CASUALTIES from Noon 30th September to Noon 25th October 1916. (At which date the Brigade left the Line)

OFFICERS:-

KILLED.

Lieut. C.S.Hipwell, M.C.	2/16th Battalion London Regiment.

WOUNDED.

Captain F.R. Rosevear.	2/13th	"	"	"
Lieut. I. Range (At Duty)	2/13th	"	"	"
2/Lieut. C. F. Burn (At Duty)	2/14th	"	"	"
2/Lieut. S. E. Jones.	2/14th	"	"	"
2/Lieut. A. D. Lane. (At Duty)	2/15th	"	"	"

OTHER RANKS:-

UNIT.	Killed.	Wounded.	Missing.	Total.
2/13th Battalion L.R.	7.	34.	1.	42.
2/14th -do-	10.	45.	-	55.
2/15th -do-	6.	27.	3.	36.
2/16th -do-	7.	30.	-	37.
179th Machine Gun Co.	-	1.	-	1.
179th Light Trench Mortar Battery	-	1.	-	1.
	30.	138.	4.	172.

Accidental etc. Wounds included in above total.

2/14th Bn. London Regiment.	1.
2/15th -do-	1.
2/16th -do-	1.
179th Machine Gun Co.	1.
	4.

Confidential

Vol 6

War Diary
of
179th Inf. Bde. Hdqrs.
for
November 1st – 30th 1916

Instructions regarding War Diaries and Intelligence Summaries are contained in F. S. Regs., Part II. and the Staff Manual respectively. Title Pages will be prepared in manuscript.

WAR DIARY
or
~~INTELLIGENCE SUMMARY~~ 98

(Erase heading not required.)

Army Form C. 2

Place	Date	Hour	Summary of Events and Information	Remarks and references to Appendices
RIBEAUCOURT				
	Nov. 1st		The Commander-in-chief inspected 2/13 - 2/15 - and 2/16 Battns - while passing through the area -	98
	2nd		Very wet day - Battns - continued practising the attack - Orders received for Bde. to move Westwards -	98
	3rd		The Brigade moved westwards to BELLENCOURT area just East of Abbeville - Units billeted as follows:-	
			Brigade HdQrs } T.M. Batty } BELLENCOURT.	
			2/13 Battn. } M.G. Coy } VAUCHELLES.	98
			2/14 - BUIGNY.	
			2/15 FRANCIERES	
			2/16 { BELLENCOURT / MONFLIERS	
			A fine day - but windy.	

1875 W: W593/826 1,000,000 4/15 J.B.C. & A. A.D.S.S./Forms/C. 2118.

Instructions regarding War Diaries and Intelligence Summaries are contained in F. S. Regs., Part II. and the Staff Manual respectively. Title Pages will be prepared in manuscript.

Army Form C. 2

WAR DIARY
or
~~INTELLIGENCE SUMMARY~~ GL

(Erase heading not required.)

Place	Date	Hour	Summary of Events and Information	Remarks and references to Appendices
BELLENCOURT	Nov. 4th		G.O.C. visited Battns. in their areas - Progressive training commenced -	GL
"	5th		Progressive Training continued.	GL
"	6th		Small percentage of 'leaves' allotted to Bde - for Officers and men to proceed home to England for four days -	GL
"	7th		Progressive Training and refitting of Brigade continued.	GL
"	8th		- do - -do- -do- -do-	GL
"	9th		Brig. Genl. H.M. Edwards arrived to assume command 179th Bde. in place of Brig. Genl. E.W. Baird - who relinquishes command -	GL
"	10th		Brig. Genl. E.W. Baird proceeds home to England -	
"	11th		Small tactical exercise carried out with M.G. Coy + T.M. By. without troops -	
"	12th		Tactical exercise without troops - C.O's. 2nd's in Command	

1875 Wt. W593/826 1,000,000 4/15 J.B.C. & A. A.D.S.S./Forms/C. 2118.

Instructions regarding War Diaries and Intelligence Summaries are contained in F. S. Regs., Part II. and the Staff Manual respectively. Title Pages will be prepared in manuscript.

WAR DIARY
or
~~INTELLIGENCE SUMMARY~~ GS

(Erase heading not required.)

Army Form C. 21

Place	Date	Hour	Summary of Events and Information	Remarks and references to Appendices
BELLANCOURT			and Company Commanders attend.	GS
"	13th		Orders received for ~~part~~ of Brigade (less Sig. Sect and 179th M.G. Coy) to entrain at LONGPRÉ en route for MARSEILLES and SALONICA.	See of Orders attached Appendix
"	14th		Entrainment of Bde. at LONGPRÉ station commenced. Very much delayed by shortage of ramps at Station	GS
"	15th		Brigade en route for MARSEILLES.	GS
"	16th		— do — — do —	GS
"	17th		Brigade assembled at MARSEILLES – Units in following camps:– Bde Hd. Qrs, TMB, 2/13, 2/16, 2/15 } CARCASSONE; 2/14. MOUSSIÈRE; Transport of All Units } FOURNIER	GS

1875 Wt. W593/826 1,000,000 4/15 J.B.C. & A. A.D.S.S./Forms/C. 2118.

Army Form C. 2118

Instructions regarding War Diaries and Intelligence Summaries are contained in F. S. Regs., Part II. and the Staff Manual respectively. Title Pages will be prepared in manuscript.

WAR DIARY
or
~~INTELLIGENCE SUMMARY~~ 9S

(Erase heading not required.)

Place	Date	Hour	Summary of Events and Information	Remarks and references to Appendices
MARSEILLES	18th		Brigade rested at MARSEILLES. All ranks confined to camp.	9S
	19th		First Transport left MARSEILLES for SALONICA.	
			Following Units on board. Bde. Hd. Qrs Sig. Sectn.	
			2/13 Battn	
			2/16 Battn	
			2/15 Battn (Less 2 coys. & Hd Qrs)	9S
			2/4. Fd. Coy. RE. and CRE.	
			2/4. Fd. Ambce.	
			H. M. T. TRANSYLVANIA. sailed at 7.30 p.m.	
AT SEA	20th		At sea	9S
	21st		— do —	9S
	22nd		H.M.T. TRANSYLVANIA arrived MALTA	9S
	23rd		H.M.T. TRANSYLVANIA remained at MALTA delayed by weather etc.	9S
	24th		— do — — do — — do —	9S
	25th		— do — — do — — do —	9S
	26th		— do — — do — — do —	9S

Army Form C. 2118

Instructions regarding War Diaries and Intelligence Summaries are contained in F. S. Regs., Part II. and the Staff Manual respectively. Title Pages will be prepared in manuscript.

WAR DIARY
or
~~INTELLIGENCE SUMMARY~~ 9/8

(Erase heading not required.)

Place	Date	Hour	Summary of Events and Information	Remarks and references to Appendices
At Sea	27th		H.M.T. TRANSYLVANIA sailed from MALTA. at 9.30 am	9/8
	28th		At Sea	9/8
	29th		At Sea. H.M.T. MEGANTIC arrived Salonica with 2/14 & part 2/15 on board.	9/8
Salonica	30th		H.M.T. TRANSYLVANIA Arrived Salonica and disembarked. while Brigade less Machine Gun Company went into DZUMA Camp on MONASTIR road. 179th M.G. Coy. arrived on 1st Dec. and joined Bde. at DZUMA camp.	9/8
			APPENDICES.	
			XXV 179th Inf. Bde Op. Order No. 23. 2/11/16	9/8
			XXVI — do — Op. Order No. 24. 13/11/16	
			XXVII Strengths at 1st and 30th Nov. 1916.	

E. Sherston Capt
Bde. Major
179th Inf. Bde

1875 Wt. W593/826 1,000,000 4/15 J.B.C. & A. A.D.S.S./Forms/C. 2118.

Appendix XXIII

179th Infantry Brigade.

STRENGTH RETURN.

As at 1st OCTOBER, 1916.

UNIT.	OFFICERS.	OTHER RANKS.
179th Infantry Brigade Headquarters:	9.	51.
2/13th Battalion London Regiment	41.	913.
2/14th Battalion London Regiment	40.	968.
2/15th Battalion London Regiment	44.	973.
2/16th Battalion London Regiment	46.	969.
179th Machine Gun Co.	10.	161.
179th Trench Mortar Battery.	4.	46.
	194.	4,081.

This Return includes Officers, N.C.Os. and Other Ranks attached from Other Units.

APPENDIX. XXV

SECRET. Copy No. 14

179th Infantry Brigade.

OPERATION ORDERS NO. 23.

THURSDAY, NOVEMBER 2nd. 1916.

Ref: LENS Sheet 11.
ABBEVILLE Sheet 14.
$\frac{1}{100,000}$.

1. The 179th Infantry Brigade will march Westwards on the 3rd November 1916.

2. Units will march in accordance with attached Table.

3. A distance of 100 yards will be maintained between Units.

4. All First Line Transport and Baggage Wagons will accompany Units.

5. Billeting Parties will meet the Staff Captain at the CHURCH in BELLANCOURT at 9 a.m. on the 3rd instant. Units will be billeted in the Villages shewn as their destination in the March Table.

6. Refilling Points will remain unchanged.

7. Brigade Headquarters will be at BELLANCOURT.
Divisional Headquarters will be at AILLY-LE-HAUT-CLOCHER.

8. Acknowledge.

E Sherston
Captain,
BRIGADE MAJOR,
179th Infantry Brigade.

Copy No. 1: Retained.
2: 2/13th Bn.L.R.
3: 2/14th Bn.L.R.
4: 2/15th Bn.L.R.
5: 2/16th Bn.L.R.
6: 179th Machine Gun Co.
7: 179th Light Trench Mortar Battery.
8: 2/4th Field Co.R.E.
9: 2/4th Field Ambulance.
10: 60th Division.
11: Staff Captain.
12: Transport Officer.
13: Signalling Officer.
14: War Diary.
15: No. 2 Coy.A.S.C.
16: A.D.M.S.
17: 60th Divisional Train.

MARCH TABLE.

NO.	UNIT.	FROM.	TO.	STARTING POINT.	TIME	ROUTE.
1.	Bde. H.Q. 179th T.M.B.	RIBEAUCOURT.	BELLANCOURT.	ROAD JUNCTION just N. of F of FRANQUEVILLE.	10.30 a.m.	ERGNIES - AILLY-LE-HAUT CLOCHER.
	179th M.G.Coy.	-do-	~~BUIGNY.~~ VAUCHELLES-LES-QUESNOY	-do-	10.30 a.m.	-do-
2.	2/16th Bn.L.R.	-do-	BELLANCOURT.	-do-	10.40 a.m.	-do-
3.	2/15th Bn.L.R.	LANCHES.	FRANCIERES.	-do-	10.50 a.m.	-do-.
4.	2/13th Bn.L.R.	PROUVILLE.	VAUCHELLES - LES-QUESNOY.	ROAD JUNCTION just N.W. of B of BEAUMETZ.	9.15 a.m.	ST. RIQUIER.
5.	2/14th Bn.L.R.	MONTIGNY.	BUIGNY.	-do-	9.25 a.m.	-do-
6.	2/4th Fld.Coy.R.E.	PROUVILLE.	EAUCOURT.	-do-	9.35 a.m.	-do-
7.	2/4th Fld.Ambce.	-do-	-do-	-do-	9.40 a.m.	-do-.

No. 2 Coy. A.S.C. will be billeted at ~~VAUCHELLES-LES-QUESNOY~~ BELLANCOURT.

A PPENDIX. XXVI

SECRET. 179th Infantry Brigade. Copy No. 14.

OPERATION ORDERS, NO. 24.

MONDAY, NOVEMBER 13TH 1916.

Ref: ABBEVILLE Sheet 14. 1/100,000.

1. The Brigade will entrain according to the attached Move Programme (marked "A"). Entraining Station will be LONGPRE. Brigade Entraining Officer:- Captain W.E.David-Devis, 2/13th Battalion L.R.

2. Units will march to LONGPRE STATION so as to arrive 3 hours before the train is due to depart. Marches will be carried out as under:-

14th November 1916.

	Unit	Starting Point.	Time of passing S.Point.	Route.
1.	2/4th Fld. Ambce.	Cross Roads EAUCOURT SUR SOMME.	11.40 a.m.	PONT REMY-LIERCOURT FONTAINE.
2.	Det.2/15th Bn. L.R.	Road Junc. N. of A in FRANCIERES.	3.40 p.m.	COCQUEREL FONTAINE.
3.	2/4th Fld. Co.R.E.	Cross Roads EAUCOURT SUR SOMME.	6.0 p.m.	Same as No. 1.

15th November 1916.

	Unit	Starting Point.	Time of passing S.Point.	Route.
4.	H.Q. 179th Inf.Bde. 179th T.M.B.	Cross Roads just S.W. of B of BELLANCOURT.	11.30 p.m. (14th inst)	Same as No. 1.
5.	Det.2/15th Bn. L.R.	Same as No. 2.	4.0 a.m.	Same as No. 2.
6.	2/16th Bn.L.R.	Same as No. 4.	6.0 a.m.	Same as No. 1.
7.	Det.2/15th Bn. L.R.	Same as No. 2.	7.30 a.m.	Same as No. 2.
8.	Det.2/15th Bn. L.R.	Same as No. 2.	1.0 p.m.	Same as No. 2.
9.	2/13th Bn.L.R.	Road Junc. just W. of V of VAUCHELLES.	11.40 a.m.	Same as No. 1.
10.	2/14th Bn.L.R.	Road Junc. S. end of BUIGNY L'ABBE.	2.30 p.m.	Same as No. 1.
11.	Det.2/15th Bn. L.R.	Same as No. 2.	4.25 p.m.	Same as No. 2.

3. TRANSPORT. All baggage will be transported to the Railway Station from Billets by motor lorry. The number of lorries allotted to each Unit will be notified later. Lieut. F.D.C.MacLagan, 2/14th Battalion London Regiment, is detailed to be in charge of these lorries and will report to Brigade Headquarters at 8 a.m. tomorrow, the 14th instant. All remaining surplus Transport in possession of Units will be returned as per attached Schedule marked "B".

4. RATIONS. Troops will entrain with rations as laid down in this Office No. S/Q/62/12 dated 13th November 1916.

5. LOADING PARTIES, etc. Attention is called to Standing Orders for transport by rail issued under this Office S/Q/62/1 dated 11/11/16.

6. ENTRAINING OFFICER. Each Unit will detail 1 Officer and 2 N.C.O's to report to R.T.O., LONGPRE Station, three-quarters of an hour before the arrival ofx their own Unit at Station.

7. ENTRAINING STATES are to be prepared in duplicate. One copy will be handed to the Brigade Entraining Officer at LONGPRE and the duplicate will be retained and handed to an Officer of the Brigade Staff at the Detraining Station.

8. Orders regarding the movement of Machine Gun Co. and Signal Section will be issued later.

9. All details surplus to the establishment who are not being taken Overseas, are to remain in their present billets until they receive orders from Division. Captain C.O.Spencer Smith, 2/16th Battalion London Regiment, will be in charge of all these Details. Captain C.O. Spencer Smith is to report to Brigade Headquarters at 9 a.m. tomorrow (14th instant) to receive instructions for rations etc. for these Details.

10. Acknowledge.

E Shuster

Captain,
BRIGADE MAJOR,
179th Infantry Brigade.

Issued at 8.45 p.m.

Copy No. 1: Retained.
2: 2/13th Bn.L.R.
3: 2/14th Bn.L.R.
4: 2/15th Bn.L.R.
5: 2/16th Bn.L.R.
6: 179th Machine Gun Co.
7: 179th Light T.M.Battery.
8: 2/4th Field Co.R.E.
9: 2/4th Field Ambulance.
10: 60th Division.
11: Transport Officer.
12: Signalling Officer.
13: No.2 Coy.A.S.C.
14: War Diary.
15: A.D.M.S.

179th Infantry Brigade.

Programme of Move.

LONGPRE TO MARSEILLES.

Unit.	Train.	Place.	Time of Departure.	Date of Departure.	Accommodation.					Remarks.
					Off.	O.R.	Horses.	4 wheel.	2 wheel	
2/4th Fd.Amb.	1st Train Type T.C.	Marche H.T.14.	6.17 p.m.	14th Nov.	11	409	67	3	-	HALTES DE REPAS during joutney.
60th D.A.C. (Part)					1	20	-	11	12	1 hour at MONTEREAU 9 hours from LONGPRE.
2/15th Battn. (Part).	2nd Train Type T.P.	Marche H.T.17	9.27 p.m.	14th Nov.	23	280	24	-	Lewis Guns.	¾ hour at MACON 12 hours from MONTEREAU.
60th D.A.C. (Part)					1	30	-	28	10	1 hour at PIERRELATTE 9 hours from MACON.
2/4th Fd.Co. R.E.	3rd Train Type T.C.	Marche H.T.20	12.27 a.m.	15th Nov.	7	237	25	-	-	From PIERRELATTE to MARSEILLES is 8 hours
Bde.Amn.Col.					3	108	136	2	18	
R.F.A.batty.	4th Train Type T.C.	Marche H.T.2.	6.27 a.m.	15th Nov.	5	140	135	1	26	Entire journey is estimated to take 45 hours.
179th T.M.B.					4	46	-	-	8	
180th T.M.B.					4	46	-	-	8	
179th Inf.Bde. H.Q.					8	40	21	-	-	
R.F.A.Batty.	5th Train Type T.C.	Marche H.T.5.	9.27 a.m.	15th Nov.	5	140	135	1	26	
H.Q.,R.F.A. Bde.					5	49	48	1	5	
2/15th Battn. (Part)					4	50	-	-	-	

Unit.	Train.	Place.	Time of Departure.	Date of Departure.	Accommodation.					Remarks.
					Off.	O.R.	Horses.	4 wheel.	2 wheel.	
2/16th Battn.	6th Train				39	959	24	-	Lewis Guns.	
2/15th Battn. (Part)	Type Special 1 First 47 Covers 2 Brakes.	Marche H.T.8.	12.26 p.m.	15th Nov.	4	210	-	-	-	
2/13th Battn.	7th Train				39	960	24	-	Lewis Guns	
2/15th Battn. (Part)	Type Special 1 First 47 Covers 2 Brakes	Marche H.T.14.	6.17 p.m.	15th Nov.	4	210	-	-	-	
2/14th Battn.	8th Train				39	960	24	-	Lewis Guns	
2/15th Battn. (Part)	Type Special 1 First 47 Covers 2 Brakes.	Marche H.T.17.	9.27 p.m.	15th Nov.	4	210	-	-	-	

STAFF CAPTAIN,
178th INF. BDE.

179th INFANTRY BRIGADE.

TABLE of

TRANSPORT TO BE RETURNED.

Vehicles.	No.	To whom to be returned.	Date to be returned. Bde. H.Q.	M.G. Coy.	2/13th Battn.	2/14th Battn.	2/15th Battn.	2/16th Battn.	Animals and Harness.	To whom to be returned.	Bde. H.Q.	M.G. Coy.	2/13th Battn.	2/14th Battn.	2/15th Battn.	2/16 Bn.
Bicycles.	4	D.A.D.O.S.			12 noon 14th	2 PM 15th	noon 15th	6 PM 14th	–	–	–	–	–	–	–	–
do.	4	do.							–	–	–	–	–	–	–	–
Supply Wagons	1	Advanced H.T. Depot.		–	–	–	–	–	2 horses & harness.	Advanced H.T. Depot.						
do.	2	do.	–	–	6 PM 14th	1 PM 15th	10 AM 15th	8 PM 14th	4 horses & harness.	do.			6 PM 14th	1 PM 15th	10 AM 15th	8 PM 14th
Mess Cart.	1	do.	–		"	"	"	8 PM 14th	1 horse & harness	do.			"	"	"	"
Water Carts.	2	do.	–	–	8 PM 14th	"	"	"	4 horses & harness	No. 2 Coy. A.S.C.			9 AM 15th	3 PM 15th	12 noon 15th	10 PM 14th
do.	1	do.	–		–	–	–	–	2 horses & harness.	do.						
Field Kitchens	4	do.	–	–	6 PM 14th	"	12 noon 14th	4 PM 15th	8 horses & harness	Advanced H.T. Depot.			6 PM 14th	1 PM 15th	12 noon 14th	4 PM 14th
									1 spare H.D. horse.	do.	–	–	6 PM 14th	"	10 AM 15th	8 PM 14th

APPENDIX. XXVII

179th Infantry Brigade.

STRENGTH RETURN.

as at 1st November,1916.

UNIT.	OFFICERS.	OTHER RANKS.
179th Infantry Brigade Headquarters	9.	51.
2/13th Battalion London Regiment	43.	980.
2/14th Battalion London Regiment	41.	930.
2/15th Battalion London Regiment	46.	1,012.
2/16th Battalion London Regiment	46.	985.
179th Machine Gun Co.	8.	178.
179th Light Trench Mortar Battery	4.	44.
	197.	4,180.

This Return includes Officers and Other Ranks attached from other Units.

179th Infantry Brigade.

STRENGTH RETURN.

As at 30th November, 1916.

UNIT.	OFFICERS.	OTHER RANKS.
179th Infantry Brigade Headquarters	8	68.
2/13th Battalion London Regiment	39.	952.
2/14th Battalion London Regiment	39.	924.
2/15th Battalion London Regiment	39.	958.
2/16th Battalion London Regiment	39.	910.
179th Machine Gun Co.	10.	180.
179th Light Trench Mortar Battery	4.	41.
	178.	4,033.

This Return includes Officers, N.C.O's and Other Ranks attached from Other Units.

www.ingramcontent.com/pod-product-compliance
Lightning Source LLC
Chambersburg PA
CBHW081406160426
43193CB00013B/2120